Forward in the Fog

Forward in the Fog

A Mother's Memoir of Trusting God
with a Broken Heart

LORI D. FISCHER

RESOURCE *Publications* · Eugene, Oregon

In memory of Joe, who inspires me to keep moving forward

Contents

CONTENTS

PART 1

My son Joe, age twenty-four, is resting in his bed, unresponsive, as he has been for the better part of two days. It is late afternoon and I am sitting with him, his several guitars and his bass in their stands behind me; gray acoustic soundproofing panels line the corner of his bedroom where he records his music.

My husband Jeff and my two adult daughters, Jamie and Anna, are there, too. The four of us sing our traditional Thanksgiving hymns: "For the Beauty of the Earth" and "Now Thank We All Our God", in four-part harmony, because it is Thanksgiving Day and that is what we always do. I don't feel like singing, but it somehow seems right to do so. We miss Joe's baritone, but hope he is enjoying the music. The final lines of the hymn hang in the air: *The one eternal God, whom earth and heaven adore; For thus it was, is now, and shall be evermore.*

Then we are silent, just being present with Joe.

I hear him exhale, and I know he is gone.

I can't breathe. My heart is slowly torn in two, unnamed emotions threatening to erupt, but I do not cry. I am stunned. I have had three and a half years to prepare, but can anything prepare a mother to lose her only son? I am not prepared.

I said goodbye to him the day before, quietly thanked him for being a wonderful son, told him he could let go whenever he was ready. But still I am not prepared.

1

First Symptoms

Behold, children are a gift from the LORD . . .

—Psalm 127:3

In June of 2014 I was just back from a lovely ten days in England with my youngest daughter Anna, age sixteen.

We enjoyed London for several days, then rented a car, and I gamely faced the challenge of driving a stick-shift car on the "wrong" side of the road.

"You'll have to be the navigator," I told her. "I have to focus on driving!"

"I'll try..." She was less than enthusiastic about this responsibility, and I understood. I too am somewhat directionally-challenged, easily lost. We would have to treat this trip as an adventure, and be flexible and gracious with each other.

We drove to Oxford, where we walked the college grounds where C. S. Lewis taught, attended a Sunday service in the beautiful Magdalen campus chapel, and visited Lewis' church, his home, and his gravesite. We have always been big fans of *The Chronicles of Narnia* and other works of Lewis, so this was a meaningful and long-anticipated visit. We continued on to the Cotswolds, relishing our country walks amongst the sheep and attending a piano concert at the small but ornate St. James church (built 1627). We even took a day trip to Cardiff, Wales so Anna could visit the Dr. Who Experience.

In the process she became an expert navigator after all; we always ended up right where we wanted to be.

She'd recently had her hair cut short, which suited her petite stature and accentuated her green-gray eyes. Artistic from an early age, Anna could often be found producing handicrafts such as greeting cards she made with flowers she pressed herself, or making jewelry with beads. Sometime she even made her own beads. She learned to knit and crochet and made lovely hats, scarves, and stuffed animals.

She put together unique yet fashionable outfits from items she found at thrift stores. Her carefully-curated song playlists often became quite popular once posted online.

My older daughter Jamie had graduated from college the year before and was the assistant manager at our city's large public library, putting her administrative skills to good use. On Sundays Jamie frequently sang on the worship team at our church. Her long hair often up in a cute messy bun, she had always been both capable and fun-loving, During her pre-teen years in children's theatre, she instinctively knew everyone's lines and cues and would whisper helpful reminders when others in the cast forgot what to say or do. When she was a young teen her ballet instructor often put her in charge of the class when the instructor needed a break.

As a child, Jamie seemed to relish her role as big sister, directing the plays and variety shows the kids performed for us, reading to her siblings, and generally providing a happy leadership for her younger brother and sister. Where Jamie went, fun usually followed.

My son Joe, the middle kid, exemplified the saying, "Still waters run deep." Intellectual, witty, and quiet, his peers admired him and his sisters adored him.

He wasn't interested in sports, especially team sports. As a young boy he told me he didn't want to have to depend on anyone else in order to succeed. I suppose we could have pushed him into baseball or soccer, but to what end? He had friends and got along well with others. He was physically active and fit. He was happy going to the archery range and shooting at targets, riding his bike, swimming. He did take a basketball class at the local YMCA when he was around eleven or twelve and was actually pretty good at this, despite his short stature. But it wasn't a passion.

One evening as he and I were walking down the hall of the Y after his basketball class, we saw through a window a kids' martial arts class in progress. Joe stopped to watch, captivated. He seldom asked for anything, so I prompted him, "Do you want to try martial arts?"

Still staring through the window, he replied, "Yeah, I might like that."

When his basketball class ended I signed him up for John Bishop's Kajukenbo class, and he never looked back. He had found his thing. He spent the next eight or so years pushing himself to the limits of his physical endurance in Kajukenbo, and he loved it.

He had high standards of behavior for himself and others, to the point where as teens Jamie and Anna teased him by naming an imaginary podcast, "Moral Adventures with Joe". Jamie assumed her best British accent as she introduced the show: "Welcome to Moral Adventuhs with Joe. In this episode, Joe reminds us one should not poke one's sister with a pencil."

Joe had decided after one semester that college was not for him, so he was working hard in order to pay rent, save money, and figure out what path to pursue. A talented musician and songwriter, he spent much of his limited free time writing and recording music in his bedroom studio.

At twenty years old Joe was working three part-time jobs: he was a courier for an escrow company, he did construction work for a family friend, and he was the worship music leader at a small church in a nearby town.

Coming in from work one afternoon he stopped to chat with me.

"Hi Mom."

I looked up from loading the dishwasher. "Hi Honey. How was your day?"

"It was okay. It's weird though—I'm having some trouble with my hand."

"What do you mean?"

"It's like my fingers are half numb or something."

"Hm, you mean your hand fell asleep?"

"It kind of feels like that, but it's been that way for a few days. It's been hard to play the guitar. . ."

I massaged his right hand and asked if that made a difference.

"Not really. . ."

"Well, let me know if it doesn't improve in a day or two."

A few days later he mentioned having the same sensation in his right foot. "I'm not sure I should be driving; today on the way home I couldn't tell whether my foot was on the gas or the brake. I couldn't feel it."

I agreed with him about not driving, and advised him to make an appointment with our family doctor. "Maybe you have a pinched nerve or something. You may need an x-ray."

Our doctor wasn't available right away, but Joe was able to see his Physician's Assistant, Christina, the next day. Joe told her about the numbness in his right hand and foot. He mentioned that he had noticed some peripheral vision loss as well as double vision. She asked him some clarifying questions and performed a few basic neurological tests.

She then ordered an MRI scan of his head, scheduled for the following Monday.

Joe didn't feel well for the next two days and called in sick to work. He had a migraine and was nauseated.

He slept a lot over the weekend and tried to eat now and then, but nothing stayed down. He seemed to be declining since his doctor visit.

Joe was still queasy and weak the day of the MRI and didn't want to go, but I convinced him we needed to find out what was going on. He somehow made it through the ordeal and back into the car for the twenty-minute ride home, fighting nausea the whole time. He stumbled into the house and collapsed on the sofa. Crawling upstairs to his bedroom was too much to consider.

I spent the next two or three hours emptying his bowl and giving him sips of water. Finally I called our family doctor.

"Dr. Allen, Joe was in to see Christina the other day and had his MRI brain scan today. He's been really weak and nauseated and hasn't kept anything down for over twenty-four hours, even water."

Concern in his voice, Dr. Allen told me, "Take him to your nearest emergency room so he can have an IV of fluids. We don't want him to get dehydrated. I'll let you know when I receive the results of his scan."

I'm not easily rattled, but I was beginning to feel uneasy...

I called my husband Jeff at work to update him, then drove Joe to our local community hospital.

In the ER, Joe was given an intravenous line which supplied both fluids and medication to control his nausea. He was asked about his other symptoms, then admitted as a patient and taken away for further scans while I waited anxiously, prayed, and updated Jeff and the girls.

The next day I decided to let our friends know what was going on, so they could support us in prayer.

Wednesday, 6/25/14
Facebook post: Lori

For those of you who know Joe (my son, age 20), I wanted to let you know that he has been admitted to the hospital. He has had issues with partial numbness on his right side for a couple of weeks, in addition to frequent headaches/nausea and some limitations in his peripheral vision. He has had 3 MRIs so far and they show lesions on the left side of his brain. He also had a lumbar puncture last night and is scheduled to undergo several more tests today and tomorrow. The doctors don't have a diagnosis yet, but we will keep you posted. We will start a Facebook page just for updates for those who want to follow his progress.

I stayed at the hospital overnight and will be heading back there for the remainder of today. He is very weak and tired and has asked that we hold off on visitors for the time being.

This is a stressful time for all of us and we very much appreciate your prayers for Joe's health, as well as for peace, courage and wisdom.

The word "lesions" meant nothing to me, but the hospital doctors were obviously concerned and performed and repeated many scans and tests on Joe at all hours. While Joe was undergoing these tests, I called Jeff and the girls to keep them informed of all that I knew.

I spent the next few days and nights in Joe's hospital room. My smart, strong, muscular son was weak and nauseated and needed me to be there with him. I found myself in the new role of advocate: asking questions of the doctors and nurses, taking copious notes, fetching food and drink when Joe was able to eat.

I was exhausted but didn't want to leave. I wanted to be near him. I did eventually go home at night once or twice that week to sleep, but I constantly wondered what was happening with Joe at the hospital, and I returned first thing in the morning in case he needed me.

Around the fourth day I asked Joe, "Would you rather be alone for a while? I know you like solitude and I don't want to crowd you."

"No, it's comforting having you here. Also it's easier for me if you listen to the doctors and ask them questions. I'm too tired to talk to them much, and I might forget things. I appreciate you taking notes to help us remember stuff…" His voice trailed off as he closed his eyes to rest.

The doctors—specialists of all types—came and went and performed their tests all week. They ruled out Multiple Sclerosis, stroke, meningitis, parasite, Guillain-Barré, and several other ailments.

Finally they admitted, "We're baffled."

At the end of the week we were still at our small local hospital with no diagnosis. Julie and Maria, two of my friends who happen to be nurses in two different states, each began gently but firmly telling me Joe needed to be transferred to a larger, better-equipped hospital.

With Maria's help I began the process to have him transferred to a large university hospital about forty minutes from our home. I later found out that several events had to line up in order for this transfer to take place as quickly as it did: a bed had to be available in the right unit in this busy hospital, case managers and doctors had to agree to the transfer, etc. I'm pretty sure Maria had to call in professional favors to make it all happen.

The doctors at our local hospital were very supportive and signed off on the transfer. The head neurologist met me at the nurse's station as I was filling out discharge forms. He handed me his business card. "Would you mind letting me know when you have a diagnosis? I am very interested in Joe's case. I have a son his age…"

I agreed to inform him when we had answers.

By late afternoon Friday Joe was settled into his new room at the University of California in Irvine Medical Center Hospital, where he would spend the next five days.

2

Where Are You, God?

I will say to God my rock, "Why have You forgotten me? . . ."
—Psalm 42:9

The doctors at UCI performed all the same tests Joe had endured at the smaller hospital. They had better equipment and wanted to research Joe's case from the beginning. Several CT scans, spinal taps, neurological tests, EEGs, constant blood work and countless MRIs later, in addition to echocardiograms and an angiogram, we still had no real information.

During that week, our good friends Buzz and Maria met Jeff and me at a restaurant across the street from the hospital and treated us to dinner. We were tired, stressed, and overwhelmed, and just sitting on the patio with them on the warm summer evening for a couple of hours, taking time to eat and trying to process what was happening, was an invaluable gift.

We would soon find ourselves surrounded by a community of caring people, many of whom we'd never met. Within the next few weeks, hundreds would contact us via Facebook to express support and offer words of comfort.

While in the hospital, Joe and I both realized we would have to accept the fact that I could not help him do everything. He hated calling for a nurse every time he wanted to change positions or make his way to the bathroom. But I was not strong enough to support him. He was weak from nausea and began having trouble with balance; the numbness in his right foot made walking still more difficult. The staff wrote "fall risk" on his chart and told him not to get out of bed without calling for a nurse.

This dependence on others was a new experience for him. He had always been the one to help others in need. I knew it must have felt humiliating for him to be so helpless, but he did his best to cover his frustration with humor.

UCI is a teaching hospital, which meant Joe had excellent care and there was modern equipment available, but it also meant medical students and interns were coming in at all hours to interview Joe and perform simple neurological tests—the same tests the attending physicians had already performed. These activities assessed his balance, strength, and dexterity, among other things.

"Can you touch my finger and then touch your nose? Can you go back and forth like that?" "Push against my hands as hard as you can" (They were usually impressed with his strength). "Tap your thumb and forefinger together over and over." "Close your eyes and hold your arms straight out in front." (Joe always failed that last one; his right arm would float upward and away from the other one without him realizing it until he opened his eyes).

They asked him about his vision, his moods, his activities, and assessed his cognition: "What day is it?" "Do you know where you are?" One doctor leaned over him and questioned him loudly, as if Joe were hard of hearing. I saw a flicker of irritation in Joe's eyes, but he restrained his emotion and answered the doctor's questions evenly.

Once while a nurse was checking his vital signs, she asked him, "What's the one most important thing we can do to facilitate your comfort?"

He replied honestly, "Minimize the number of times I have to repeat myself."

I chuckled inwardly, while hoping he hadn't come across as rude. He assumed it was a straightforward question and he gave a straightforward answer. He meant no disrespect, and when he learned that answering the same questions from different doctors helped them gain a clearer picture of his situation, and that the medical students were required to practice these tests on real patients, he didn't mention the issue again.

One afternoon a hip young man in jeans and a sport coat strode in to Joe's room and declared, "Well, they want me to do a biopsy."

Noting our blank stares, he smiled and introduced himself as Dr. Abram, a brain surgeon, then proceeded to tell us that a craniotomy would help the medical team isolate the problem. "I'll remove a small sample of the abnormal brain tissue to be examined in a lab. This will lead to a definitive diagnosis."

His confidence put us at ease somewhat; I don't think either of us in our fatigue fully comprehended the seriousness of brain surgery and the risks involved. But we understood that it was necessary in order to have answers and to move ahead with some sort of treatment, so after discussing it with his dad and me, Joe signed off on the procedure.

We didn't have a diagnosis yet but I knew things were not good. It didn't help that nurses gave us looks of pity but avoided giving us pertinent information about Joe's case. It was obvious to me they knew more than they were allowed to share with us. When I pressed for details, they answered vaguely and assured me, "I'll let the doctor know you have questions." I didn't fault them for following the rules, but it was frustrating being kept in the dark.

My good friend Maria, a busy professor of nursing, stopped by to drop off homemade cookies for Joe and to take me down to the cafeteria for lunch. I had been subsisting mainly on granola bars and trail mix for several days. She admonished, "This is going to be a marathon, not a sprint. You need to eat. And you need to rest when you can."

Her marathon comment concerned me—perhaps she also knew (or suspected) more than I did? I was too tired to question her.

The night before the surgery, I stayed with Joe in his hospital room. We were still stressed and exhausted from the uncertainty of the situation and our lack of sleep. I didn't even have the energy to read to Joe, and we didn't have internet access, but I found a one-hour Brian Regan show in my downloads and Joe and I watched it that night on my laptop.

We hadn't laughed in a long time, but Brian made us laugh, again and again, providing a wave of relief from our bleak and uncertain circumstances. I was filled with gratitude for the talent and drive God has given to some people that allows them to entertain us. Even those who don't acknowledge the source of their talent can be a blessing.

The hour of laughter didn't change our situation; it just provided a ray of sunshine on the dark road. But it was a good reminder to stay open to humor and to search it out often. Good comedy isn't just frivolous; it can be healing in a way, and a road to a fresh perspective. It certainly helped us, if only for an hour.

Later, weary with the weight of the unknown and the lack of sleep, I paced the hospital halls at three a.m. while Joe dozed. Sadness, confusion, and fear took over and the floodgates opened—I ducked into a bathroom, sat on the trash can and sobbed uncontrollably, my head in my hands. I don't know how long I sat there, trying to pray through the tears but unable to find words. Worried and frightened, I longed for any sign of God's presence and care, but He seemed so far away, and silent. Was He ignoring us? Or did He see us suffering and not care?

> *When you pass through the waters, I will be with you;*
> *And through the rivers, they will not overflow you.*
> *When you walk through the fire, you will not be scorched,*
> *Nor will the flame burn you.*
> *For I am the LORD your God,*
> *The Holy One of Israel, your Savior...*
> Isaiah 43:2–3

Between sobs, I choked out broken phrases, rocking back and forth.
Oh God . . . where are You? . . . Where are You?! . . .
But You are good . . . You are good . . . I know You are good . . .
Through tears I reminded myself what I knew about God in spite of my feeling abandoned by Him: He is good. He cares. He is near. He knows what is going on and He has a plan. His ways are higher than mine.

The LORD is compassionate and gracious, slow to anger and abounding in lovingkindness... Just as a father has compassion on his children, so the LORD has compassion on those who fear Him. Psalm 103:8, 13

The LORD is righteous in all His ways and kind in all His deeds. The LORD is near to all who call upon Him, to all who call upon Him in truth. Psalm 145:17–18

For as the heavens are higher than the earth, so are My ways higher than your ways and My thoughts than your thoughts. Isaiah 55:9

Joe was taken in to surgery late the next morning. Jeff called to say he would take the rest of the day off to come to the hospital and wait with me, but I knew there were issues at work that required his attention, and Maria was already there with me, so I suggested he finish out his work day. I sensed I would need his presence and comfort many times in the near future and wanted to be sensitive to the load he was carrying as our family's provider.

Monday, 6/30/14, 3:30pm
Facebook post: Lori

They said Joe should be out of surgery by 6:00. It's very hard not to as-sume the worst and I am certainly on edge. He seemed to be dealing with it well today, quiet for long periods but also answering the countless questions with patience and humor. He daily asks how I'm doing. I'm trying not to break down in front of him as he has enough to deal with! But I know he knows how tired I am and has probably heard my voice crack when I choke back tears.

I need my son. Please ask God to let me keep him for a long, long time.

The six-hour surgery went fine, and Joe was discharged to go home the next day. I spent the next week and a half in a state of limbo, trying to keep things as normal as possible at home while longing for a call from a doctor to discuss the results of Joe's brain biopsy. We wanted to start mov-ing ahead with whatever we needed to do to fix the problem. I called once or twice that first week, but was told, "I'm sorry, we have no information for you at this time. The doctor will call you, hopefully within the next few days."

During this waiting time, Joe wrote the following on his blog:

I'm feeling the need to do something important right now. The world is sinking, guys. I am not unjoyful, but I am in earnest. I have it on my heart to tell someone something, someone who will listen. I'm often more stringent on myself, a stickler, a prude. Why? Because it is brought home to me, and I want it to stay brought home to me that the world, if it matters, matters desperately. With the gift of a moment of clarity, how can I tell you how much I love you for being human? How can I tell you how much you matter? Win you over to your own side? His side? Does this make sense to anyone?

Joe was weak and had trouble walking. Besides the effects of whatever was happening in his brain, he had almost no feeling in his right foot. But he was up and about for short periods each day and took very short, slow walks with Jeff or me after dinner, using a walker or a cane for support. The hospital had sent him home with a walker, which he reluctantly used for a day or two before ditching it. He much preferred to walk unaided and did so as soon as he was able. The cane was a necessary compromise.

Double vision meant that reading was nearly impossible, so he asked us to read to him. He had been reading *Surprised By Joy* by C. S. Lewis, so he and I finished that one first. He'd been a "thinker" almost from birth; his choice for our next books were *Orthodoxy* and *The Man Who Was Thursday,* both by G. K. Chesterton. I had to stop now and then to ask him to explain things to me. Although he said his brain was "fuzzy", it seemed to me his intellect was still sharp. He understood concepts and deeper meanings in literature, he was just having a hard time articulating them, perhaps because of his fatigue and weakness.

He also sometimes asked us to read the Bible to him. "I do have an audio version but the speaker reads too fast—it's hard for my mind to keep up. If one of you is reading, I can adjust the pacing by asking you to slow down."

Joe knew many people were praying for him because of my Facebook updates, and one afternoon when he felt well enough, he decided to address these friends himself:

Wednesday 7/2/14, 1:00pm
Facebook post: Joe

Well hi, everybody.

You all know the story . . . I guess there's really not much to say except thank you for your prayers. They show your love for myself, my family, and the Lord Himself. This is the Church in her glory.

My current challenges are as follows: I have poor control over my right leg and arm; it's like they're partially asleep. So no driving, no guitar, and no torch-juggling . . . Stuff like that is out. This has led me to wonder—well frankly what I'm going to be good for in the next few weeks or possibly longer. Anxiety and restlessness, I have no doubt, will be coming for me.

However, I have good health and my Lord, Whose grace has brought me safe thus far and Whose grace will lead me home.

Nine days after the above post, I received the call that would change our lives forever.

3

Joe Responds

Whom have I in heaven but Thee?
And besides Thee, I desire nothing on earth.
My flesh and my heart may fail, but God is the strength of my heart
and my portion forever. —Psalm 73:25–26

"Mrs. Fischer, this is Doctor Garcia. We have the results of your son's biopsy. I would prefer to have this conversation in person, but since you've called several times I wanted to get back to you right away. I'm sorry—the news is not good. Joe has a stage four brain cancer called glioblastoma multiforme…his tumor is inoperable…"

He continued on about it originating in the brain and other details that meant nothing to me at that time. My heart was in my throat and my head was pounding.

After I hung up I poured out a desperate prayer for help, then went to find Jeff, who was working from home that day. I relayed everything the doctor had told me, and we sat together for a few moments, stunned.

Together we told Joe, who took the news in stride. He was solemn, but there was no evidence of fear or anger, or even surprise. We discussed the doctor's recommendation of combined radiation and chemotherapy and mentioned the probable side effects. Joe wondered aloud what the benefits of such a treatment would be. Jeff explained, "it's our best chance at slowing down or even shrinking the tumor, and will most likely extend your life and mitigate tumor-related side effects, like seizures." Joe agreed to move ahead with the recommended protocol, but I couldn't help wondering whether it was more for our sakes than for his.

7/11/14 5pm
Facebook post: Lori

> *Joe has Stage 4 brain cancer.*
>
> *It is called glioblastoma; it originated in the brain and is very aggressive. We will know more about treatment options and what to expect in the near future once we meet with the neuro-oncologists on Wednesday. They were kind enough to return my call today once they had the pathology report, but said they prefer to talk further specifics in person . . .*
>
> *We have been dealt a terrible blow, but we are not knocked out. Make no mistake—we are shaken to the core. But God is bigger than cancer and we trust His plan. Please continue to walk with us. We need you.*

My Facebook update generated dozens of responses of shock, sympathy, and promises to pray for Joe. I savored each response and read them over and over. However, the next day Joe posted his own response to the outpouring of sympathy:

7/12/14 9:30am
Facebook post: Joe

> *Ok. Here's my piece. Listen up.*
>
> *What I've got is a big, bad, for all I know green and purple stage-four tumor-goober fooling around on the inside of my noggin.*
>
> *Who cares?*
>
> *Now, I am really grateful for all the sympathy I've received—I am. I hope I don't hurt anyone's feelings by taking this so lightly, but guys, pull yourselves together. Do you know what matters to me today? Hearts. Do you know what mattered to God yesterday? Hearts. Do you know what will matter to God tomorrow? Guess. (It's hearts).*
>
> *Guys, I have a wish. I have a dying wish and it's the same whether I die today of cancer or in five decades of a stroke. If anybody is willing to do anything for me ever, do this for me today: Make my joy complete by being*

of the same mind, maintaining the same love, united in spirit, intent on one purpose.[1] *What else has ever mattered anyhow?*

7/16/14 8:45pm
Facebook post: Lori

Thank you so much for your prayers for our appointment with the on-cologist today. We had a long visit—Dr. Garcia spent over an hour with us, explaining things, showing us scans, answering our questions. The prognosis is not good, but those of you who looked up glioblastoma already knew that.

The doctor confirmed that Joe's tumor is inoperable, so we will start ra-diation and chemotherapy shortly in an effort to slow down its growth and possibly shrink it. He will undergo both types of therapy simultaneously for six weeks, then have a two-week break (during which time we hope to get away as a family for a few days) before continuing on with chemo for one year.

We don't know yet whether Joe is a candidate for clinical trials, but we will certainly chase down any opportunity we can find. We already have calls in to UCLA's top-rated neuro-oncology program.

As you continue to pray for healing (it would really have to be a miracle), please also be praying for minimal side effects, not only from the therapies he will soon undergo, but also from the drugs he is taking now (anti-seizure and anti-swelling). He says they affect his mood and make him irritable, although we have seen very little evidence of that! He keeps himself in check very well. I'm sure I wouldn't be half as gracious if I were in his shoes.

Joe continued to feel weak and was unsteady on his feet, but he hated feeling useless. He stayed busy helping around the house with the garden and other light work. He cleaned out kitchen drawers, repotted plants, and continued to do his own laundry.

He also played chess whenever he could find a willing opponent. He felt his cognitive abilities had decreased recently and wanted to keep his mind sharp. Unfortunately for him, I was often the only one available dur-ing the day, and I wasn't much of a challenge.

He sometimes tried to help me. "Are you sure you want to move your queen that far? And if you castle, your king won't be so vulnerable."

"Um...ok, what's castling?"

---

1. This was in reference to Bible verse Philippians 2:2.

"It's when you move your king laterally two spaces and your rook jumps over it."

Even with his patient coaching, I still lost almost every game.

He felt compelled to tender his resignation at both of his regular jobs: the escrow company courier position and the worship leader position. Both employers were sorry to see him go—he was a dependable and responsible employee and was well-liked by those with whom he worked. Kerry, his boss at the escrow company, assured him that he would keep his job open for him and told him to take as much time off as he needed, but Joe somehow knew that he would not be able to return, and advised Kerry to fill the position with someone else. It was the first of many, many losses Joe would experience in the months to come.

Around this time he came up to me one day and handed me his driver's license.

"I guess I won't be needing this anymore."

I replied with something like, "You never know—with treatment and therapy, you may regain some of the abilities you've lost. Anyway, you'll still need it for identification, so keep it in your wallet for now."

When the license expired a few weeks later on his twenty-first birthday, he didn't even attempt a renewal; he simply applied for a state-issued photo ID card.

4

Aphasia

*Why are you in despair, O my soul? And why have you become
disturbed within me? Hope in God, for I shall again praise Him
for the help of His presence. —Psalm 42:5*

8/3/14 10pm
Facebook post: Lori

*We went to a Tim Hawkins concert tonight. Joe wanted to stay home but we
talked him into going with us. We regret that. The concert was great, but Joe
was exhausted and had a bad headache when we got home. Not enough dinner, too many people and stairs and waiting in lines, being out of the routine
. . . I think he knew how it would affect him but made the sacrifice because I
wanted us to do something fun as a family. Lesson learned: Joe knows himself.*

Joe began radiation treatments in early August, about a month after
his diagnosis. It took that long to make appointments, get evaluations, have
his radiation mask made, and wait for authorizations and prescriptions to
arrive.

The day of the third session, we stopped at the lab to get his blood
drawn (an unpleasant weekly necessity) before going on to his radiation
appointment. He had a headache throughout the morning, but powered
through the procedure. Immediately after his treatment he became sick to

his stomach. He rested at the clinic for a few minutes, then gingerly got into the car and we started home.

About two minutes later he asked if we could stop the car for a while as it felt better to him to just have everything completely still. It was a hot summer day, but I found a shady spot in a small parking lot and we rested in silence for about half an hour before heading home.

The next morning I went into his room to help him get ready for his radiation appointment. I was not prepared for what I encountered.

He looked at me and tried to speak, but he couldn't seem to get words out, and when he did venture something it made no sense. Obviously disconcerted, he waited while I called his doctor, who told me to call an ambulance and get him to the hospital.

An MRI showed that the tumor had grown into the speech center of his brain and was causing swelling and hydrocephalus. Joe was quickly scheduled for surgery the following day to install a shunt in his brain to drain the excess fluid and relieve some of the pressure caused by tumor activity. His doctor also increased his corticosteroid dose to reduce the swelling in his brain.

The steroids made Joe feel weak and tired, which was especially frustrating for my strong, fit, black-belt son. But he knew they were probably saving his life, so he took all of his medications faithfully.

8/13/14 6:30pm
Jeff (Joe's dad)

Joe just got out of surgery. Dr. Abram's first words to us were, "boy did he need that shunt!" His intracranial pressure was double what it should have been, and was undoubtedly the source of the lethargy and confusion. Now it's a race between the tumor's growth and healing from the surgery, since we can't restart radiation until his surgery wound is healed.

8/14/14 10:30pm
Jeff

This is a tough one to write. We met with one of Joe's neuro-oncologists today, and she laid out the situation from her perspective. The tumor has grown considerably faster than most she's seen (she called the growth "very rare", and named the tumor "a monster"). While the shunt has restored some of his cognitive ability, the tumor has grown into his speech center. Only a physical shrinking of the tumor plus speech therapy holds any chance of restoring his ability to express himself beyond the simple "yes" and "no" type of responses he is currently capable of. He's obviously frustrated with this, time and again trying to get us to understand him, but with only very limited success. His fate—as is all of ours—is in God's hands.

8/15/14 8:45pm
Lori

I hardly know what to write. It has been a horrendously painful few days as we have had one blow after another. Yesterday at the hospital I could barely talk without choking up. But we are home now and that is always more restful and comfortable.

As you know, Joe currently cannot say much more than "yes" and "no", but tonight at dinner he motioned that he wanted me to switch places with him. After we switched seats he said, "no" and motioned for Jamie to switch with him. He then said, "henceforth" and smiled. So I guess we have a new seating arrangement, after years in the same places. I have no idea what that was all about, but we found it amusing. Wonder if he'll remember tomorrow.

We have lots of appointments in different cities in the weeks to come (for instance on Monday we'll get his labs drawn locally, then drive to Fountain Valley for a CT scan, then on to Anaheim for his radiation treatment), so I would appreciate prayer for peace and clear thinking (and energy) for me and that Joe would tolerate the full schedule and the treatments well. He does get tired very easily these days . . .

Our pastor and several lay leaders from our church came over tonight and we had a great time of prayer for Joe. The road we are walking sometimes feels excruciatingly rocky and dark, but knowing you all are walking alongside us is more comforting than you can ever know.

Tonight Jeff was helping Joe into bed and couldn't figure out why Joe wanted to lie with his head at the foot of the bed. Finally he realized Joe was asking for the curtains to be opened so he could see the sunset!

Joe loved watching sunrises and sunsets, which may have started when he was very young and I walked him to the park in the gray predawn so he could sit at the top of a big slide and see the sun come up. (Trees and houses on our street precluded a good view of sunrises). I don't remember whether it was his idea or mine. But he was rewarded that morning as the sky changed colors and the sun appeared over the hill in all its brilliance. At his request we did that several more times together until he was old enough to walk the neighborhood by himself.

8/16/14 10:00am
Lori

Several new words this morning: "again", "plural" and "weird". When I asked whether he wanted milk or juice, he thought for a moment then said "again". I realized he couldn't find and repeat the words for milk or juice but he could say "yes!" when I repeated "milk".

He motioned for me to sit down at the table with him and asked, "plurals word or plural words?" I told him the right answer, then he seemed to want me to explain the concept of plural. I showed him with one napkin in one spot and several napkins in another spot. He said "Ohh . . . that's weird . . . "

Joe spent the next few days working hard to recover his ability to communicate. I had never heard of aphasia, but I was getting a close-up lesson. He needed to reconnect each idea with its spoken word. He knew the idea he wanted to express and he often knew the word to go with it, but he couldn't make his mouth cooperate with his brain. Neither could he transfer the idea to his hand, so writing, typing, and sign language were not accessible either.

Can you imagine being locked inside yourself, unable to communicate? I can't. But it must be a very scary place indeed.

We did have charts with pictures on them, thinking he could point to a picture to communicate, but he didn't use them. To this day I'm not sure why. Were the pictures confusing? Or did he simply feel the activity was too juvenile for him? Or something else? I wish I had asked him later why he didn't seem to want to use the charts at that time, but I didn't remember it until recently.

8/18/14
Lori

No real changes from yesterday, but it is so heartening to see Joe really trying to find the words he wants and to communicate with us. It's difficult, but he seems patient with himself as he works at it and now and then he'll come up with the word he wants, or one of us will guess the right word and he'll brighten up and say "YES!" I have no doubt he remains my intellectual superior.

We had been told that the only hope for Joe's recovery of speech was a physical shrinking of the tumor along with speech therapy, neither of which had happened yet. In fact, the tumor had grown since Joe's first MRI, just a few weeks prior. But we watched in delight as he slowly and laboriously worked his way back to fluency. He discovered he had whole phrases still accessible from his memory, such as lines from favorite movies ("Roast chicken! My dear Sam…"[2]).

8/21/14
Lori

I cannot get over how much improved Joe is—it really is remarkable. One week ago he had about three words at his disposal: yes, no, and bang. (He's still trying to remember what that last one meant, but he used it a lot!). Today he is conversing normally, only occasionally searching for the word he wants (much like I do!), even using his typical catch phrases like "no worries" and "cool beans". We were all set to schedule speech therapy, but he really doesn't need it now. We talked about it today; he said he feels like he willed himself back to language ability. I could see all week that he was working hard at it—he would get our attention, then sit and think for a moment, then venture a word or something that sounded like a word and look at us questioningly. We would respond accordingly. Once we guessed the right word he would have us say the word slowly so he could practice repeating it. It was pretty fascinating, really.

Once, he asked his sister Jamie, "What's that good-tasting thing…?"
She ventured a few possibilities: "Bacon? Tacos? Pie?"
Bingo! He wanted her to make an apple pie for him. She did.
Joe was constantly fatigued from his medication, and when he was especially tired his speech slowed and he would mix up words like "wife" and "mother" or "he" and "she". But after a few weeks he was able to communicate normally once again—one of many blessings we experienced during his cancer journey.

2. From the Peter Jackson film, *The Two Towers.*

5

Nutrition and Health

Then God said, "Behold, I have given you every plant yielding seed that is on the surface of all the earth, and every tree which has fruit yielding seed; it shall be food for you.

—*Genesis 1:29*

Almost immediately people began giving us advice about nutrition, supplements, and alternative therapies. I didn't mind at all; I soaked up the suggestions and appreciated the input. I had always tried to feed my family meals that were both healthy *and* yummy, but that became an even more focused mission now.

One of the most common assertions was that cancer feeds on sugar, so Joe should stop eating sweets. This was hard to accept, because Joe loved desserts. He would often ask one of his sisters to bake him a pie or a cake, and they always gladly complied. Apple pie was his favorite. When I explained that he probably shouldn't be eating sugar anymore, he was disappointed but agreed to do his best to avoid it.

I began to experiment in my baking, substituting refined sugar with healthier sweeteners. I had many disappointing results but several successes, too. Even today I have no idea whether our sugar avoidance was an over-reaction—there is so much conflicting advice regarding cancer and nutrition, and one can find so-called experts on either side of the sugar issue.

Joe had always relished food. I continually questioned my judgment regarding Joe's nutrition, and every now and then reminded him, "These decisions are yours to make. I may have opinions about nutrition, but you're an adult and you can eat what you want." I didn't want to be responsible for making his life less enjoyable.

He would always respond with something like, "Yeah, I know. But you do all the research so I appreciate your advice. I may not always follow it, but I still want to hear it. It helps to know what I *should* be eating and avoiding."

So we soldiered on.

I heard that juicing was vital to Joe's health, so I started talking about getting a juicer. My sister Lynn sent us an excellent one, and I daily juiced leafy greens and other produce for Joe. He dutifully downed everything I gave him, even the barely palatable (too much kale). Fruit has sugar, so I focused on raw vegetables with a green apple and maybe a few berries thrown in. And some of the juices were actually quite good.

He cut back on red meat and dairy, because it seemed the healthy thing to do. Ironically, Joe really needed to *gain* weight, not lose it (he was 5'7" and barely 120 lbs. at this point), so on the advice of his doctor we incorporated high-quality protein shakes and exercise to build muscle and stimulate hunger.

Our insurance provided both physical and occupational home therapies for Joe twice a week for two months. His therapists told him to be sure to do his exercises every day, even when they were not there to work with him.

Joe told me, "It's a lot easier for me to do this stuff when there's someone here to coach me. I'm too tired and unmotivated otherwise." So we incorporated forty-five minutes of rehab exercises into our schedule on the days he didn't work with the therapists. We used free weights, resistance bands, and a balance board our neighbor Jim made for him. On two or three occasions we even practiced—slowly—some swing dance steps Jamie taught us.

Once the home therapies ended, we hired a personal trainer to come to the house for a few weeks to help create a good workout routine for him. Joe did his best to follow his trainer's advice daily, but some days he just didn't have the energy.

It was a constant challenge to make sure he took in enough calories but also kept to a healthy diet. Perhaps we could have found a qualified cancer nutritionist to help us with these decisions, but it all seemed to work out. With the exception of a long bout of bronchitis (or maybe pneumonia—we never did get a conclusive diagnosis) early in his journey, he mostly stayed healthy, even dodging many of the colds and flus that made the rounds in the community each year.

The above-mentioned bronchitis caused much discomfort for Joe for about six weeks throughout October and early November that first year: fever, coughing that prevented him (and me) getting a good night's sleep, and even greater fatigue than usual. He wasn't able to put much effort into his rehab exercises during that time. He went through two full rounds of strong antibiotics to no avail, then had a bronchoscopy that showed nodules on his lungs. It wasn't clear to his doctors what the problem was, but they mentioned possibilities like tuberculosis, a parasitic infection, even cancer.

Around this time I began researching the use of herbal supplements. I sought and received advice from a naturopathic doctor and settled on several high-quality whole-food supplements, which Joe willingly took by the handful twice a day. They were to support his blood, liver, and immune system throughout his cancer journey, especially important while he was taking chemotherapy drugs.

We also started using essential oils, such as frankincense and oregano. Joe's doctors were supportive of our complementary efforts and just wanted to be kept informed of what we were using at home. If they were dubious about the efficacy of these additions they kept those opinions to themselves. The lead neuro-oncologist, Dr. Covachi, even pointed me to an app from Memorial Sloan Kettering that describes hundreds of herbal supplements and the research associated with their use in cancer patients.

Whether as a result of the alternative treatments at home, or just from the passage of time, or the direct touch of God's hand, Joe's lungs finally cleared up without further medical intervention. This was yet another of many blessings we experienced along the road.

6

Community

Oil and perfume make the heart glad,
so a man's counsel is sweet to his friend.

—Proverbs 27:9

8/24/14
Lori

There is an older couple we often chat with in the waiting area at the radiation clinic, Cecilia and Walter. Cecilia told us she has breast cancer but her prognosis is good. She is from Guatemala and came to the U.S. when she was fifteen because her father wanted to find a better life for his family. She and Walter met on a blind date.

They admire Joe and his calm attitude about his diagnosis. Please pray that we will provide words of life and hope and that they will see Christ in us and want to know more.

Although this Facebook group is about Joe, this paragraph is about me. Because of the road we are walking with Joe, I am learning first-hand about the beauty of community. I have a rather independent personality; for many years I truly believed I would be perfectly happy living alone away from human society. The Spirit of God is correcting me and I am being brought face to face with my own self-centeredness and pride. Your prayers, encouragement, advice, practical help, gifts, meals and myriad other expressions of love and grace are overwhelming at times and certainly humbling. Thank you for being instruments of His mercy.

Joe, like me, had an independent spirit. He got along well with people and seemed to be liked and respected among his peers. But he invested his energies more in serving the public than in developing personal friendships. About two years before his diagnosis he and I were taking one of our evening walks, and I asked him about his finances and what his goals were for the near future. He admitted to me that he often stopped to chat with people living on the streets, and that he didn't have much money in savings because he frequently bought shoes, jackets, blankets or food for those in need. How is a mother supposed to react to that? Of course I loved his compassion and wanted to encourage it, but I also wanted him to plan for his future. I wanted him to be discerning about his surroundings and stay safe.

Motherhood—for me at least—is a constant balancing act: what do you say and what do you keep to yourself? And when do you worry and when do you relax and let go?

Although Joe and I had much in common, I think we may differ here: he didn't seem to require much company or interaction with friends during his season of suffering. Granted, during his cancer journey he was virtually always fatigued, and socializing requires energy.

His friend Chrissy joined us once or twice at the infusion center and quietly played guitar and sang with Joe—a ray of sunshine in a rather dreary place. Other friends of his from church made themselves available and once, about four or five of them stopped by to visit with him—they sang worship songs and talked and joked and prayed with him. He really seemed to enjoy it, but as far as I know he didn't reach out to request more visits and when I offered now and again to set something up, he declined. Perhaps he felt deprived of these social visits and declined only because of fatigue, or maybe he just didn't feel the need for them. Either way, once his health began to wane, he seemed to be satisfied with the social interaction provided by his family.

But during our long days and nights at the hospital, whenever Joe was sleeping or just resting and lost in his thoughts, or whisked away for yet another scan, I found myself wishing for company. Jeff often drove the forty-five minutes after a full day at the office to join us in the evening, and sometimes offered to come during the day, but I knew he was needed at work. Joe's friend and mentor Bob stopped by during that first confusing week and visited with Joe while I stepped outside for some fresh air. On one occasion our friends Rick and Laura came to sit and pray with me for a few minutes, and I so appreciated their company. And Maria made herself available to meet me at the hospital for lunch at times or sit with me during Joe's surgeries.

It sounds like a lot as I write it, but I do remember often feeling cold and alone during Joe's hospitals stays. I should have reached out and asked people to visit. Although Joe usually wasn't up to having company, I would have enjoyed having someone to talk with in the family waiting areas or walking the grounds outside. In the same vein, I should have brought flowers in to his hospital room—not that he would have cared, but they would have cheered me.

However, many, many people ministered to our family in the months soon after Joe's diagnosis, which was the most confusing and stressful time. Neighbors and church friends delivered meals, picked up groceries, gave gas gift cards (we were doing a great deal of driving between home, the hospital, radiation appointments, and the rehab center), donated essential oils; one brave soul even gave Anna a driving lesson to help her prepare for her driver's test. My sister Lynn and my brother Dave each visited from out of town, as did my childhood best friend Laurie.

I was both touched and humbled by the outpouring of support. I had never had a problem serving others in need, but in my pride I had come to believe I didn't really need people. I was wrong.

7

A Birthday and Blessings

For we are God's handiwork, created in Christ Jesus to do good works,
which God prepared in advance for us to do.

—Ephesian 2:10

Joe turned twenty-one the summer he was diagnosed with brain cancer. I
offered to invite some friends over to help celebrate his birthday; he considered it for a few days, then decided to forego a party for a quiet family
barbeque. Jeff and Jamie harvested apples from our backyard apple tree and
Jamie baked a birthday pie for him. Our neighbors Tim and Jill stopped by
with twenty-one mylar balloons, and we realized once again how thoughtful our neighbors are. (Some of them provided meals for us on busy days,
our neighbor Jim built a balance board for Joe to use for rehab exercises,
and neighbors we had never met introduced themselves to us and began
asking about Joe whenever we ran into them on the street).

Many people posted birthday greetings to Joe on Facebook that year;
following is a sampling:

Happy, Happy, Happy Birthday Joe!!!!!!! Thank you for being a friend
and prayer partner to my husband Bob. You inspire him and challenge him
spiritually, and he is so honored to know you. One day, early into your diag-
nosis, you spoke to the Men of church at their Saturday morning meeting just
to share where you were at. When he came home I asked him how it went,
and he just said, "All us old geezers just got schooled by a 20 year old. He was
a blessing." Our entire family has grown to love you through your relationship

with Bob, and we diligently pray for you and for God's healing to touch that noggin' of yours. Have a very blessed birthday today! —Sue

Happy 21st birthday, Joe! We miss seeing your smiley face each day at the escrow office! You are always in our thoughts! Hope your day is filled with songs sung by Anna, pies made by Jamie, shoulder massages from your mom, and a challenging game of chess with your dad. It's the simple things in life that are most enjoyable. —Kerry

Joe received a nice mic for his birthday, and that week he felt well enough to return to the "studio" (in his bedroom) to remix a few of his previously-recorded songs and to begin teaching Anna how to use Logic Pro, Apple's music production system. He even recorded the whole family just for fun—singing hymns, if memory serves.

He continued to improve that summer and was able to walk freely—with a slight limp—when in the house. At our request he used a cane for extra support and balance when outside. Nausea came and went but usually was not much more than a slight queasiness. This was exacerbated by hunger, so he tried to remember to eat a snack between meals if he felt hungry. We also saw great improvement in his speaking—such a relief to us all! —as the effects of aphasia dissipated. He and Anna and I joined a local no-frills gym, to add variety to our respective workout routines.

Throughout his teens Joe was constantly improving himself. Whether perfecting his guitar-playing, his writing, his martial arts ability, or studying the Bible, he remained both student and teacher, usually at the same time. But it seemed to me he pursued excellence with even more fervor after he began losing abilities in speech, cognition, and movement; he never stopped trying to mitigate his limitations. While he faced the diagnosis (and prognosis) with acceptance, he did not accept the associated limitations easily. I suppose that is how he most ardently "fought" cancer. He fought the effects even more than the inevitable result.

9/3/14
Jeff

Today was a long day, a tough day, and an encouraging day. Long because Joe had radiation in the morning, then an appointment with the neuro-oncologist, then his first infusion with the new drug (Avastin). He and Lori left the house at 10 a.m., didn't get back until around 6 p.m. I joined them for the doctor visit. Tough, because as we discussed the course of treatment with the doc, she reminded us once again that from a medical perspective, this tumor is incurable. Both chemo drugs will eventually stop working. But it was also an encouraging day because Joe's progress verbally and physically has now been officially classified as "amazing" by UCI's head neuro-oncologist (M.D., Ph.D.). She is very careful and conservative with her assessments, so to hear the "a-word" from her was quite something. There is still no firm medical explanation for his recovery of these abilities, and when I suggested divine intervention, she replied, "hey, I'm not going to argue with that." And then added, "Don't argue with a miracle, Mr. Fischer."

So thank you over and over for all of your prayers. We are so enjoying this time with Joe, just seeing him able to pretty much take care of himself, as well as able to enjoy his passion for playing and recording music at a substantial fraction of his pre-cancer state. We of course want this to continue, and of course want it to be permanent. The latter will obviously take a miracle, so we humbly ask that you continue to pray with us toward that end. But in the meantime, please be encouraged that your prayers are having a very obvious effect.

Toward the end of that summer our dear friend Jerry raised funds among our friends and family members to send us on a family vacation. He must have known we needed the time to just enjoy each other as a family, away from medical issues. Once the doctors signed off on the idea, we happily discussed possibilities. Joe loved sunsets so we made "great sunsets" priority number one. Priority number two was "no airports". When we found a house for rent online that was right on the beach, with a full wall of glass facing the ocean, we knew we had found our home-for-a-week in Morro Bay, California, a half-day's drive from our home.

We spent a pleasant week in early October playing on the beach, exploring the town (and the charming neighboring town of Cayucos), sitting on our patio playing guitars and watching the waves roll in, and enjoying many lovely sunsets. We returned home refreshed and rested. This thoughtful and generous gift provided well-timed comfort for us, as well as lasting memories. It served to remind us to keep our focus on the bigger picture: God is always good and He is always at work in the lives of those who love Him. Our job is not to decipher His logic; our job is to trust Him.

8

The Statement

The steadfast of mind You will keep in perfect peace,
because he trusts in You.

—Isaiah 26:3

10/15/14
Joe

'Ello folks. I'm chilling in the waiting room waiting (imagine that) for my turn in Star Tours' latest and greatest: the MRI machine! If you see this in the next few and feel like praying, here are a few things you can ask for: Hardware/ software that works properly; Focus and peace for the staffers, techs, what have you; A complete lack of coughing and other head cold symptoms; Good attitude for me no matter what; And, if it's what God has in mind, no tumor. Peace out and bless someone today. Thank the next vet you see; they appreciate that.

When Joe was three years old, six-year-old Jamie led him in a prayer to ask Jesus into his heart to be his Savior. As he grew up, he attended church with us and participated in family devotions.

Early in his teens, he developed depression. Evident in many of his poems from that period is a general sadness and dissatisfaction with life. For a while it was sometimes difficult for me to find a way to connect with him, and at times it seemed to me he was rather easily irritated. He stayed under our doctor's care and took medication to balance his serotonin levels.

He was well into his teens when he began to "own" his faith in God.

Later, he told us that late one night, he strongly sensed God speaking to him, convicting him of a certain habitual sinful behavior, conveying something along the lines of: "You call yourself a Christian and yet behave as if you are not Mine. Make a choice, Joe. Are you going to follow Me or not?"

Joe knew God loved him and had sent His Son to pay the penalty for his sins, and overwhelmed by God's grace he surrendered and told God, "I am Yours." He made a conscious decision, clarifying and cementing the choice he made at three years old, to trust in God and in His goodness and to follow His ways.

He still generally kept his thoughts and emotions private, revealing them most openly in his songs and poems. But the Holy Spirit was working on him, and after his midnight encounter with God, he was a changed man—he became both more confident and more gracious. The last few years of his life he seemed to possess a remarkable peace and sense of purpose in spite of his declining health. The sullenness of his early teens was gone forever.

The Spare Room

I always found comfort in sadness
It seemed only then things were true
But after trying to fight it
I finally decided
There's room for happiness, too

© Joe Fischer 2014

He had written "A Name for Me" soon after he made a commitment to follow Christ (before he knew about his cancer). Our pastor had just preached a sermon on the second chapter of the book of Revelation, which includes these words in verse 17: "To him who overcomes…I will give a white stone, and a new name written on the stone which no one knows but he who receives it." The white stone may allude to an ancient practice of giving such a stone to those declared innocent after a trial (a black stone was given to those found guilty). Or it may refer to another ancient practice of presenting a white stone to the victor of an athletic event, inscribed with the winner's name.

On this particular Sunday, we each found a white stone on our seat; Pastor Brian asked each of us to write a name on our stone that we wanted to represent us (perhaps something like "Beloved" or "Joyful"). He encouraged us to keep the stone as a reminder of who we are in Christ.

One of the verses of Joe's song states: "If Your plan has a part for me, I will gladly see it through; if tomorrow sends me home, well, I would rather be with You".

> Chorus to "A Name for Me"
> If You want to call me 'Conqueror'
> That's not too much—that's what I'll be
> If You want to call me 'Child'
> That's not too small a name for me
>
> © *Joe Fischer 2013*

Joe's Christian faith showed through even in his pop-style love songs, such as "Bulletproof". This is a song about unrequited love. It's a sad message, but the bridge says: "And no, I won't be staying home; I've got two lives to live and none I own." Written long before his cancer diagnosis, the song addresses the reality and the anticipation of the next life, in heaven. In those few words, he also admits submission to his Savior: even this life doesn't really belong to him, it is a gift from God.

He had traveled throughout his teen years, usually with groups from our church: Jamaica at age fifteen, Ethiopia at seventeen, Moldova at nineteen.

On our mother-son trip to Ireland when he was sixteen, we explored the wilder west coast from Dingle to Westport, and even spent a day out on the lonely Achill Island. We both were moved by the sense of history and desolation as we passed one abandoned farmhouse after another, remnants from the famine of the 1840s.

After his trip to Eastern Europe in 2013, he wrote on his blog his thoughts about finding joy and purpose:

I knew on the flight into LAX that, if it was here, it was going to be hard to find, and I was right. I haven't yet despaired of finding it, but I've come close. I've come close to forgetting that I want it. But there's a hill by my house and every time I walk up, I remember. When I'm outside, the lid has been taken off, and a hot cloud of thoughts billows up until my head is cool again.

On the trip, with the team was Heaven. 20-some people I didn't know, but loved. I didn't even like being around some of them for too long, but I loved them. I loved them, not because of the specific personalities they had, rather, in spite of those personalities, I loved them because they were my team. And the choice of love led to the phenomenon of enjoyment. I enjoyed what I did not naturally like.

Ever wonder if God's real? What if He actually is? Kind of changes the status quo. On the trip, we assumed that God was. We attended either to Him, or to each other in ways explicitly prescribed by Him, out of love for Him, in obedience to Him. The effect? Pleasure was joy, pain was joy, energy was joy, fatigue was joy, even a sadness sharper than I'm used to was joy.

Why not here in my own community? On the trip, we were predisposed to use every opportunity, even to look for opportunities to do the right thing. Over here, we're predisposed in other ways. We're predisposed to pursue educations, careers, homes, friends, lunch. We're not seeking evil, we're just not seeking good. I'm not seeking good.

It's been proven to me that joy exists. I was thrown into its ocean for three weeks. Freely soaked. Ashore and dry, I have nothing forcing me to believe in joy, but no excuse to disbelieve. Consider this my promise to keep looking.

I had been told to be prepared for a personality change as a result of the tumor; anger, anxiety, and confusion are not uncommon among brain cancer patients. There were changes that were more of a physical nature: Joe spoke more slowly and moved more slowly than before. But the only personality change I noticed during most of his illness was a stronger focus on spiritual matters and on important things like love, generosity, and personal discipline. He became even more determined to find ways to serve people, to show the love of God in practical ways.

He instituted a nightly family prayer time, when we would each share with each other how we were doing and what we needed prayer for. Then we would pray for each other. After a few weeks we changed it to once a week, and it was always a special time.

Although the residual effects of aphasia sometimes left him with a decreased vocabulary, he often started conversations with people we met at the radiation center or in the infusion clinic waiting area. They would share why they were there, he would say "Can we pray for you?" And when they agreed, he would motion for me to take the lead and do the praying because he didn't want to make them uncomfortable when he couldn't find the words he wanted.

It was the same story when he saw a homeless person while we were out—he would ask me to pull over, he'd walk up to them, say "hi" and introduce himself, then wait for me to take over and converse with the person. When he wanted to start volunteering twice a week at Food for Life, a local food distribution center, that meant I was there volunteering alongside him.

Some of these experiences were not ones I would have chosen on my own, but I loved being with Joe and always felt honored not only to be his driver and companion, but also to witness first-hand how he doggedly served the public—without reservation—in spite of his physical and even mental limitations. He pulled me out of my comfort zone and I am better for it.

During one of our family prayer times, Joe shared with us a big idea he'd been mulling over for several months. At the edge of our town, there is a three-story, 50,000-square-foot commercial building that had been standing empty for over a year. Joe dreamed of starting a non-profit outreach ministry in that building. He planned to recruit several others to live and work there with him. It would be a music venue, as well as a place for people living on the streets to eat, rest, and have open and honest conversations with people who care about them.

Meals would be served to anyone who needed one. He and his band would perform free concerts there on weekends. At the end of each concert he would invite people to the local church for the following Sunday service; the staff would give them rides.

It was to be a residential facility and anyone who wanted to live and eat there would also learn marketable skills, attend Bible studies, and have regular chores. The organization would provide referrals and rides to affordable mental health services as well as rehab programs for substance abuse addicts.

On one of his many hikes in the local foothills, he had come across a boulder on which someone had spray painted "make a statement". This became the inspiration for the name of the outreach. It would be called The Statement, and Joe envisioned those words emblazoned across the building, like a beacon. The entire effort would be Joe's statement to a hurting world: there is hope, and it begins with God.

He didn't know the first thing about the details of such an undertaking or whether there was even a need for such a thing in our area, and his life was cut short before he could explore the possibility of making his dream a reality. But if God had given him more time here on earth and if He had confirmed this plan, I'm quite sure Joe would have pursued it with the same passion and determination he brought to his music, his martial arts, and to the people he already served.

9

Finding a Routine

Do not fear, for I am with you;
Do not anxiously look about you, for I am your God.
I will strengthen you, surely I will help you,
Surely I will uphold you with My righteous right hand. —Isaiah 41:10

1/1/15
Lori

Strange to think about the year just passed. One year ago brain cancer was the furthest thing from our minds. In June our lives were turned upside down. There have been moments (days, really) of agonizing stress as well as moments of incredible blessing and delight. God is constant and faithful through it all, and I can't imagine going through this experience without Him. He is the only true source of peace. Joe shared his perspective tonight at dinner, and hopefully he'll share it with you soon. But we all feel that God is preparing Joe for a more effective ministry. We look forward to 2015 with complete trust that God is integral to this adventure and that He is working in our family.

As I have mentioned before, we have also come to appreciate in a fresh way the value of friendship. Both Joe and I are very comfortable with solitude. It is easy for me to neglect relationships because I enjoy my own company so much—ha! Thank you for coming alongside us, commenting, praying and helping. You are all very special to us—the rocky parts in this road are less burdensome with you here and the pleasant parts are more fun when shared with you.

Happy New Year. May 2015 find you drawing closer to your Creator, taking Him at His Word and enjoying His friendship most of all.

After six weeks of daily radiation therapy to stun the beast, we fell into a routine that took us through the next two years: weekly lab draws, bi-weekly visits with the oncologist, which Jeff always attended with us, twice-weekly visits to Casa Colina Rehab Facility for physical and occupational therapy, regular MRIs (generally every six weeks), and bi-weekly "thirty-minute" infusions at the cancer clinic, which usually involved several hours of waiting.

Although the chemo drug Joe was prescribed—Temodar—was a pill he could take at home, he also was prescribed the drug Avastin via infusion in an attempt to starve the tumor. Each month he took the Temodar for five days, feeling more lethargic with each succeeding day. Several days of recovery followed, during which his strength and energy gradually returned. He would typically have about two weeks of relatively good days before beginning the process all over again.

We learned that the standard treatment for glioblastoma—radiation, Temodar, and Avastin—had not changed in several decades. Once these drugs stop working, and they virtually always do, there aren't a lot of options. One problem is that chemotherapy drugs that work well against cancers elsewhere in the body do not cross the blood-brain barrier, making them ineffective against brain cancer. Additionally, glioblastoma has the ability to mutate and adapt to whatever is thrown at it; perhaps that is why Dr. Covachi called it a "monster."

But Joe's doctors were confident the treatment would give him more time (the average lifespan at the time was fifteen months with treatment vs. four months with no treatment), and the hope was always that something better would be discovered in his lifetime.

Several friends told us about a news story they'd heard recently about a clinical trial being held at Duke University for glioblastoma patients. We asked Dr. Covachi about it; she said these tests at Duke had been going on for years and she was constantly watching them and others (including UCLA, also on the cutting edge of cancer treatment) to determine what Joe might be eligible for and when. Most of them had to do with recurrent GBM (meaning the cancer had diminished and then come back more aggressively) and Joe was not in that category.

Joe frequently had both physical and occupational therapy, but he seemed to do best when he was pushing himself on his own terms: taking walks, working out with weights, practicing his martial arts forms with Anna, playing guitar and drums, etc. Our black spaniel Roxie often joined him on the treadmill. Normal life activities were his main therapy.

The weekly lab draws were irksome but necessary. Joe often didn't feel great, and I imagine having his inner arm pricked with needles so often was irritating. He tried to remain upbeat, but whenever he winced I could almost feel the pain myself.

Years later, we found the following on his computer; we're not sure when he wrote it:

> (To the tune of *Bicycle Built for Two*)
> Blood draw, blood draw
> Count up my platelets, do
> My white blood cells
> Should be included too
> I'll try not to spill the urine
> I see the stress that you're in
> So stick me once (but please not twice)
> And I'll try not to yell when you do

My role as advocate continued as I found myself maneuvering—sometimes subtly, sometimes not—to get the best therapists, the best infusion nurses (there were a couple that I didn't want anywhere near my son, given their hesitation with the needle and the many times they failed to find a vein; there were others who were wonderful and competent and I was always relieved when one of them was available), and even the best dental hygienist for his regular dental checkups.

Once when I stayed overnight during one of his hospital stays, he was weak and nauseated, drowsy with medication. An aide came noisily into his room around 3 a.m., opening cupboards and banging the doors shut. We awoke, startled. When she discovered Joe's incontinence, she berated him loudly. "Why didn't you get up and use the bathroom?! You made more work for me!"

Joe quietly apologized, "I'm sorry… I was asleep…"

Wide awake now, I was furious, but held it together while she did her work so I wouldn't embarrass Joe, and so she wouldn't take out any more anger on him.

As soon as she left, I stepped out to find Mary, the head nurse on duty that night. I was shaken but I was on a mission. I relayed to her what had happened and stated, "I do not want that aide to step foot in Joe's room ever again. She is not to be near him."

Mary listened carefully, concern on her face. "Thank you for telling me—you did right to report this. There is no excuse for that behavior; I am so sorry. We nurses don't see how the aides treat the patients because we are not in the room at the same time. I'm very sorry. I will take care of it."

Thankfully we didn't see that aide again.

The "mama bear" in me was always near at hand to overpower my natural timidity when necessary.

Joe never wanted me to make a fuss, so usually I tried to keep my missions covert. I was always walking that fine line: pushing for the very best for him but not making him the focus of the situation, usually not even letting him know what I was doing. I'm not sure whether my interventions made much of a difference, but at the time they seemed crucial to me.

But I Don't Feel Brave

They said I was strong
But I didn't feel strong
I felt weak and tired and confused

They said I was brave
But I didn't feel brave
I felt nervous and stressed and afraid

They said I was wise
But I sure didn't feel wise
I felt bewildered and overwhelmed
As I scribbled notes during doctor visits
And researched available options
And cried out to God for help

Feelings are not the point.

© Lori Fischer 2018

In between the medical appointments and hospital stays, we celebrated birthdays and other holidays, ate dinner together when we could, celebrated Anna's graduation from high school, moved Anna to Nashville for a year so she could study audio engineering and music business at a working studio, played a lot of music, saw Jamie buy her first car, moved Anna back home and saw her achieve her own black-belt status (both Joe and Anna studied Kajukenbo for many years), attended church each week, watched Dodger baseball, walked our sweet spaniel every day, chatted with the neighbors, and just generally lived our lives together. Jeff and Joe began taking a short evening walk on Saturdays after dinner.

We had instituted "Family Night" many years prior; on this evening once a month we ate dinner together, shared a short devotional time, and played a game or did some activity together. We took turns choosing dinner, leading the devotional, and choosing the after-dinner activity. Even as the kids grew up and moved out, at their insistence we maintained Family Night; it was on everyone's calendars and we each made it a priority. Joe liked playing cards, especially Hearts, so we often played that when it was his turn to choose the activity. Or we would get out our instruments and jam together.

For his birthday dinners, Joe often requested pulled pork sandwiches. I added slaw to round things out, and there was always pie for dessert.

Besides the Temodar and Avastin, Joe was on anti-seizure meds, anti-nausea meds, and the steroid Decadron. All of these drugs have proven benefits as well as unwanted side effects. His doctors regularly made minute adjustments according to the need. We learned that Temodar slows tumor growth but suppresses the immune system, causes fatigue, and lowers platelets—Joe's low platelets caused occasional nose bleeds and once or twice he required a platelet transfusion. Decadron reduces inflammation and pressure on the brain, and can curtail nausea, but causes muscle weakness (Joe hated this) and can impair wound healing (especially important after surgery).

One afternoon right after a platelet transfusion in the infusion center, he had a bad reaction: he suddenly developed severe chills and shivered uncontrollably. Even wrapped in several blankets he couldn't get warm. He kept three nurses and a doctor busy for the next half hour. They gave him Benadryl and a steroidal breathing treatment, as he was coughing so much they thought he might be having trouble breathing, too.

The staff was wonderful: alert, competent, and kind. I was relieved when things calmed down enough for us to go home. He thanked the nurses and made a couple of his customary light-hearted comments, which seemed to put them at ease.

Although Joe never appeared fearful or angry about having cancer, the constant fatigue and muscle weakness annoyed him. He wanted to go on living his life as he always had, and seemed to consider cancer a nuisance more than anything else.

The days he felt he hadn't accomplished anything were especially frustrating. He pushed himself when he could: he gave guitar lessons to the neighbor kids, helped with the gardening—both at home and in the neighborhood—, continued doing his own laundry and helping with household chores, and spent time writing songs and recording his music.

He had recorded and released his song "No Good Reason" just a few months *before* he was diagnosed with an inoperable brain tumor.

> I remember the day I was given this journey
> The day I was shown to this door
> I remember the day, I just can't recall life before…
> © *Joe Fischer 2013*

The song (available on Apple Music and Spotify) concedes that from our limited perspective, sometimes there seems to be no good reason for why things happen as they do. As my friend Judy said, the lyric was prophetic.

10

Forward in the Darkness

Sing to the LORD a new song;
Sing to the LORD, all the earth. —*Psalm 96:1*

Joe was a skilled songwriter and guitarist, and although the tumor greatly impacted his abilities in those areas, he pushed forward. His right hand was partially numb and his muscles weak from medication, so playing guitar was difficult at best.

Singing became more challenging, too, as he lost some of his pitch control and vocal energy. As for writing songs and poems, he told us he felt his cognition had declined and his mental skills were fuzzy. He continually fought against this by playing chess, studying languages online, working mental puzzles, and having me read to him from Chesterton and Lewis. I admired his tenacity; medication affected his attention span and it was hard for him to concentrate on anything for long. But he forced himself to keep trying.

His personal circadian rhythm often found him lethargic during the day and energetic in the evening. This was a challenge because of course his appointments were always during the day, when he felt most tired. In the evenings—when *I* was most fatigued—he was mentally alert and ready for me to read to him or play guitars together. We tried to remain sensitive to each other's needs and found a balance that generally worked for us:

usually early evening after dinner. Playing guitars with Joe was rewarding for me—he somehow made me sound better than I was.

He began stopping by our bedroom just before he went to bed each night to hug Jeff and me each goodnight. This became part of his nightly routine—I am so grateful for it.

Sometimes during those jam sessions I thought wistfully of how far he'd come as a guitarist, only to lose his skill now.

When he was around eleven years old, we gave him a three-quarter size guitar for Christmas. I had taught him a few chords and he'd been using mine to practice on, but it was too big. He used the smaller guitar for about a year. He then found and bought himself a good-quality used electric guitar. He took a few lessons from a family friend, and our neighbor Brett recommended a set of guitar theory books which Joe worked through on his own. He learned scales, theory, bar chords, and much more than I ever knew. He spent much of his free time playing and practicing guitar, always pushing himself to improve.

As homeschoolers, our afternoons were often free, so one day I took Joe and Anna to the Taylor Guitar factory in El Cajon, California, for an afternoon field trip. It was fascinating to watch the process of guitar-making, and the kids were able to play some of the finished products while there.

Throughout his teens Joe played in garage bands with Jamie and other youth from church, putting on concerts for parents and friends. One time he put a band together and arranged to do a summer evening concert on the stage at our local outdoor shopping mall. The band performed covers of hit songs as well as some of their own original music. As far as I know he made all the arrangements: communicating with the events coordinator, running rehearsals, and heading up the set-up and tear-down of mics, amps, and all the other equipment.

Joe was interested in many different styles of music. From a grand organ recital at a large church to a jazz trio in a small smoky club, he always said yes to an invitation to hear good music.

He listened to a lot of Switchfoot and Fiction Family during those years, so I would guess he was influenced by Jon Foreman, but he developed his own style as a guitarist and singer-songwriter. He bought himself a nice Martin acoustic and began leading the worship music for the Junior High department at our church. Eventually he was hired as a worship leader at a nearby church, a position he enjoyed very much. He was forced to give it up a year later when he was diagnosed with cancer and began having difficulty playing.

A year or two after his cancer diagnosis, he gave his Martin to his sister Anna, also a musician. We encouraged him not to give up playing entirely, and a few months later he bought a Taylor and resumed his efforts in making music.

While it saddened me to watch his abilities decline as he lost some control of his right arm and hand, it was also inspiring to see him continue playing and singing, even recording, as long as he was able.

Soon after his diagnosis, Joe wrote and recorded "Do I Look Scared?" He felt compelled to reassure people that he wasn't afraid.

> Chorus to "Do I Look Scared"
> Will it last? Will it ever come back?
> I have no idea
> Do I care? Does it look like I'm scared?
> I've got nothing to fear
> © Joe Fischer 2014

Further along in the same song he repeats his matter-of-fact attitude: "Could be old age, could be tonight. I suffer no loss on the day I die…"

He had loved taking long walks alone, and during his later teen years often slipped out late at night to walk the neighborhood and the local hills, to think, pray, and sometimes write songs. He wrote "Forward in the Darkness" while on one of these walks. He told me later that he was up in the local foothills at dusk when heavy fog rolled in and he became disoriented and somewhat apprehensive. Everything around him was dark and hazy—he wasn't sure which way to head. Then he looked behind him and saw that the fog had cleared enough for him to get his bearings and head in the right direction toward home. This reminded him of the faithfulness of God—even when we can't see or feel His presence, we can remind ourselves that He has always been faithful in our past and we can trust Him to lead us home.

> Chorus to "Forward in the Darkness"
> I look up and I see darkness
> Look around and I see haze
> I look back and I remember You
> So I look forward in the darkness
> To all the uncertain days
> I can't wait—I remember You
> © Joe Fischer 2014

After his diagnosis, he gave up these beloved late-night hikes (as far as I know!), although he continued taking short walks during the day. On more than one occasion, he took his guitar and climbed the local hill to sit and play music and watch the sun set. He was unsteady on his feet, even on flat ground, so hiking up the hill—carrying a guitar, no less—was extremely difficult, but he had inherited my quiet stubborn streak and was determined. When I couldn't talk him out of it, I invited myself along, staying a few feet behind in case he slipped.

11

Limitations

Behold, I have refined you, but not as silver;
I have tested you in the furnace of affliction. —Isaiah 48:10

Joe's tumor ("the beast") had its fingers in many parts of the left hemisphere of his brain, and was from the beginning considered inoperable and impossible to eradicate. One article I read described this type of tumor as "like sand in grass". The report of his first MRI—even before a definitive diagnosis—mentioned "abnormalities in the left frontal lobe, left parietal lobe, left corona radiata, left thalamus, left brainstem, left posterior pons, left occipital lobe"; these abnormalities affected his balance and coordination, speech, sense of touch, and vision, among other things.

Joe developed double vision early on. His oncologist referred him to a highly-regarded neuro-ophthalmologist, Dr. Garnier. Her cheerful disposition was contagious, her French accent lovely. I always enjoyed our visits with her. On our first visit she gave Joe a thorough eye exam and checked his latest MRI results. She told us there was a paralysis of his left eye nerve and a considerable peripheral vision loss on the right side (so, the right half of both eyes). She also said Joe was visually coping really well considering how dense the loss was.

She told Joe she could perform a simple strabismus surgery to address his double vision, but the peripheral vision loss was unfortunately permanent. He opted to go ahead with the operation, and it was scheduled for two months later. A week before it was to take place in Irvine, the anesthesiologist decided that since Joe had brain cancer, the surgery needed to be performed at the Orange facility, which was near the hospital, in case of complications. And so it was rescheduled for the following month.

This meant Joe was off both Temodar and Avastin for several weeks, as his doctors wanted him completely off these medications for two weeks on either side of the surgery; they were concerned about interference with wound healing.

Ultimately the surgery was a success and significantly reduced Joe's straight-ahead double vision, though it returned from time to time when he was especially fatigued. The loss of peripheral vision would remain for the rest of his life.

Another local medical facility, St. Jude Rehab Center, offered a Driving Assessment program and Jeff thought it would be a good idea for Joe to take part in it, just to determine whether there might be a chance for Joe to drive again. Joe consented, and the three of us spent the afternoon with the friendly driving analyst at St. Jude. The assessment included neurological and visual testing, as well as time in a driving simulator and a few minutes actually behind the wheel in a dual-controlled car. The report confirmed what we pretty much knew: modifications could be made in a car to compensate for his right-side weakness, but the peripheral vision loss precluded his driving. Joe seemed to know ahead of time what the results would be, so he was unfazed.

I was not surprised by the report either, but I was sad. Joe had already given up hiking, and the finality of knowing he would never drive again was just one more loss chipping away at his independence.

Along with all the other discomforts Joe experienced, he developed a case of shingles along the side of his face and right shoulder, and on the fingers of his right hand. This was a painful and distracting rash that persisted for about two weeks. His doctor gave him a prescription for it, but he found the greatest immediate relief using pure Aloe vera gel.

As balance was an issue and falling always a risk, Joe sometimes used a cane when walking amongst other people outside our home, such as at church. He didn't like it because he didn't want people to feel they had to make way for him; he also didn't care for the attention it drew, and he certainly didn't want anyone's pity. But he knew it was necessary—crowds were extremely difficult to navigate, not only because of the balance issues, but having no peripheral vision meant he couldn't see anyone coming up alongside him. His doctors warned him repeatedly that a fall could cause further damage to his brain and be dangerous for him.

When my father died, the five of us flew to San José for his burial service. Our local airport was crowded the morning of our flight, and we found ourselves in a long serpentine queue at the ticket counter. I suggested to Joe that I try to secure a wheelchair for him, as it might make things easier until we got to our gate, but Joe firmly declined the offer. Our queue intersected with several others, so we were shoulder to shoulder with people on all sides—people who didn't know Joe, and had no reason to be careful to not bump him with their luggage or jostle him as they pushed past.

In spite of my effort to stay close to him, at one point the four of us became separated from Joe, and as I made my way back toward him through the slowly moving crowd I saw a mixture of agitation and bewilderment in his eyes. I called to him: "Stay there—I'll be right there."

Disoriented, he replied in frustration, "Stay where?! Which queue am I in? They're all moving in different directions!"

It probably took less than half a minute for me to return to him, but it felt to me (and probably to him) like much longer. I wanted so much to hug him and reassure him that everything was okay now, but he wasn't my little boy anymore, and hugging him right then would have embarrassed him. So I satisfied myself with linking my arm in his and moving through the rest of the line that way. He didn't seem to mind; in fact, it was common for his sisters or me to link arms with him while walking together, even long before cancer affected his vision and balance. We liked being near him, and I think he enjoyed it, too.

Joe's two sisters were so good for him as they were growing up. He had a serious, introspective nature; they taught him not to take himself or this life too seriously. They didn't teach by verbal instruction, but by the way they related to him. The three of them would banter back and forth at length, playing off each other's comments—Joe loved being in the middle of this. The girls quoted movie lines (voicing the characters) and made him laugh. And his subtle throw-away lines and deadpan humor often set the girls laughing as well.

They supported his passion for music and recording by singing back-up for him or providing feedback (no pun intended) on his new songs as he shared them with us.

They savored a lot of the same books, and while they were all strong readers, Jamie loved reading aloud to them over the years. The three of them truly enjoyed each other and some of my very happiest memories are of all of them doing the dishes while singing pop songs in three-part harmony, or just lounging in the living room playing cards and making each other laugh. They did a lot of laughing.

As young adults, Jamie invited Joe to be involved in the Bible study she attended across town, at the home of our friends Scott and Marci. After his cancer diagnosis he could no longer drive, so she came over every Sunday night to give him a ride there and back.

Both Jamie and Anna are musicians as well. Jamie plays piano and sings; Anna plays guitar and sings. When Joe had to step aside from leading worship for our private school chapel time (a role he cherished) because he could no longer play guitar well and his singing voice was weak, Jamie offered to lead so he could back her up and still be involved. When she couldn't do it because of work commitments, Anna stepped in.

Joe was good for them, too. He encouraged and inspired them to develop their talents. He helped teach Anna to play the guitar—after I taught her a few chords and strum patterns, he passed on to her the more complex and intricate aspects of playing. They even did some busking together around town and at the beach. He coached her in her martial arts studies and showed her how to change the oil in a car.

He and Jamie were in the same friend group and they attended parties and Bible studies together. They led worship music together and sometimes just performed together for fun.

He was a good listener and when asked, gave good counsel. He was what my friend Jan called "an old soul," wise beyond his years.

12

Feeling Useless

Do not merely look out for your own personal interests,
but also for the interests of others. —Philippians 2:4

3/2/16
Lori

The PET scan Joe's doctors want was decisively denied a third time by the insurance company (apparently they only approve it for epilepsy) so Joe is scheduled for an MRS to give them further information about his tumor activity.
So please pray

- *for good news from the scan (scheduled for March 9)*
- *that Joe would remain healthy and strong*
- *that this season of our family's life would count for good in the grand scheme of things, and that God would use it to make us "mature and complete, lacking in nothing" (James 1:4)*

Thank you, dear ones!

3/16/16
Lori

The MRS scan went fine, except that they had to jab him several times before they found a vein for the IV. Still has a bit of bruising a week later . . .

We saw Dr. Garcia today, who went over the scan results. It indicates that the tumor is still "viable", meaning that although it doesn't seem to be growing, it still could at any time. So he recommended another twelve cycles (one more year) of Temodar. Bleh. Joe said he's up for it, as long as the dose doesn't go any higher than he's had before, as he feels that's about all he can handle. The idea behind Temodar is that it reprograms the cancer cells and tells them not to replicate. It appears to be working.

So we stay the course with Avastin and Temodar. We continue to eat with an eye toward nutrition. I just signed up for a regular delivery of local produce and my first box arrived today! I guess I'm a "greens nerd" because it was such fun going through the box and seeing all the yummy produce. Joe and I had salads then and there, with fresh romaine, French radishes (who knew?) and something called tatsoi (tasty!).

Thank you for your continual support. We are so blessed to have you in our lives, even those of you whom we've never "met." I ask that you pray as you generally do:

1. *that Joe would have an easy time of it with the Temodar*

2. *that the tumor would shrink*

3. *that Joe would continue to find purpose and meaning in this season of his life*

4. *that God's name would be lifted up in this situation and that He would receive the honor He is due*

"Who is like the LORD our GOD, who is enthroned on high, who humbles Himself to behold the things that are in heaven and in the earth?" (Psalm 113:5,6)

He is good. All the time.

Although Joe had an MRI only every six weeks, sometimes that appointment fell the same week as his twice-monthly clinic visit with his oncologist. Joe referred to these occasions as "party week": he would have his labs drawn on Monday, his MRI on Tuesday, his clinic visit on Wednesday, followed by an Avastin infusion (a long day), and perhaps a check-in with Dr. Garnier, his eye surgeon, on Thursday. These weeks were tiring for both of us and there wasn't time to do much else, but we had good conversations in the car or listened to music we both enjoyed, usually our own playlists of contemporary praise or pop music.

Throughout his cancer journey, Joe constantly sought ways to be useful. He helped the neighbors with their yardwork as long as he could. He helped at home with housework. He always came out upon my return from shopping to carry in groceries from my car. He even exercised Roxie on the treadmill, on days I didn't have the time or energy to walk her outside.

Actually, the desire to be useful and to serve others was a lifelong trait of Joe's. I kept a journal for each of my children as they were growing up; here's an entry from when Joe was seven years old:

It's just you and me tonight—Annie (age 3) is in bed, and Daddy and Jamie are out for the evening. After getting our jammies on, I built a fire and read to you in the living room for a while. When I mentioned I was tired, and hungry (you had eaten, but I hadn't), you sprang into action—took my hand and led me to the table, where I ate my salad. You asked me what else would make me comfortable. You wrote everything down so you wouldn't forget: cup of tea, pillow for my back, hug from Joe, piano music. You supplied everything so quietly and cheerfully—I felt loved and honored to be your mother! You played the beginning piano songs we've been working on together, and they sounded beautiful to me.

He longed to continue playing guitar and leading worship for his Bible study group or for the children's department at church, but the weakness in his right arm meant he couldn't keep up a regular tempo, and he knew he would be more of a distraction than an asset.

Once, during an especially tiring week, he admitted to me, "I really don't know what I'm here for. I can't do much of anything."

After thinking about that for a moment, I answered, "Maybe it's not about doing. Maybe it's about being. Maybe your purpose at this time is to be gracious and courageous as you face a difficult, unpleasant situation. People are watching you and are being inspired. Maybe that's your purpose."

That seemed to give him a sense of peace. He had been fulfilling his purpose all along.

13

Bad News

O God, You are my God; I shall seek You earnestly;
My soul thirsts for You, my flesh yearns for You,
In a dry and weary land where there is no water. —Psalm 63:1

3/8/17
Jeff

After almost two years of stable MRIs, we got a bit of bad news today. Joe's tumor showed some growth since his last MRI in December. The growth is in the left visual cortex, and although his straight-ahead vision is still ok, Joe seems to have lost even more peripheral vision on the right side, which may be due to the tumor growth. Once the doctors have more information, options include a "booster" shot of radiation, a biopsy, or even surgical removal of the affected area (the new growth is in a fairly reachable area—unlike the rest of the tumor). The latter option may also allow for typing against additional drugs, since the Temodar is apparently ineffective against the new recruit. So as always, please pray for wisdom for the doctors, and for Joe too as he weighs the options and decides which course of action he prefers.

After repeated denials and appeals, our insurance company finally approved another MRS test (Magnetic Resonance Spectroscopy), which would give Joe's oncology team needed information. While the many MRIs showed where the tumor was located, the MRS would indicate its chemical metabolism, or how aggressive and active it was.

The MRS results confirmed increased cancer activity, very unwelcome news after two years of the tumor being "alive but asleep". We met with the neurosurgeon; he assured us that the new growth was in a more reachable area of Joe's brain and had clear margins, meaning it was operable. He said any tissue samples they removed would help the team find appropriate clinical trials for which Joe might be a candidate, and that the biggest risk would have been vision loss on the right side, but Joe already had that. Joe told him, "let's do it."

4/3/17
Lori

We had a productive consultation with Dr. Morales, the new neurosurgeon, this week and have decided to move ahead with resection surgery. We very much appreciate your prayers—thank you for walking this road with us. Please continue to pray for:

1. *successful surgery and quick and complete recovery*

2. *strength and balance*

3. *improved peripheral vision (insert miracle here)*

4. *guidance and open doors regarding a career path for Joe*

We are closing the door on one season (the Temodar years) and preparing to walk through another door. I am hoping this will be the start of an exciting season of healing and purpose for Joe. But whatever comes, we know God is always good and worthy of all our praise.

Joe recovered well from the surgery. His oncologists sent some of his tissue sample to the clinical trial registry and found that he was a match for a "promising" drug called Palbociclib. It had been used with success for other types of cancer but not yet for glioblastoma, so we were in uncharted territory. He would need to be completely off the steroid medication (Decadron) in order to participate. When we saw Dr. Garcia later that week he indicated that the best we could hope for was "no new growth". But of course we knew that anything was possible.

Joe was only too happy to reduce the dosage of his steroid medication because it made his muscles feel weak, which led to him feeling unproductive. We cautiously cut back on the Decadron. The next day he had a headache and was nauseated. The day after that he appeared at my office door while I was sitting at my desk. He just looked at me and made a sound, like "hmm….". My heart dropped. Aphasia was back—once again he had lost the ability to speak.

For anyone to lose the ability to speak, read, and write is a serious and discouraging thing. But for a songwriter-poet, it must be especially disheartening, to be trapped inside oneself, unable to express thoughts in a way people understand. What happens to that creativity when it cannot be expressed? When the poet's soul is alive and active but mute?

I called his doctor, who told me to increase the steroid back to what it had been, and that we could review the situation at his regular clinic visit in a few days. Joe's headache and nausea abated, but communication remained a problem for several more weeks. And because he could not tolerate decreasing the steroid, much less going off it completely, he was no longer a candidate for the clinical trial with Palbociclib. Temodar had stopped working. The beast was waking up, and we were quickly running out of ammunition.

14

Growing Weary

My soul weeps because of grief;
strengthen me according to Your word.

—*Psalm 119:28*

It was gratifying to watch Joe work so hard to regain his ability to speak. He would point to something and gesture for me to say the word, watching my mouth carefully. Then he would try to repeat it, often with limited success.

As before, writing, typing, and sign language were not options, as he couldn't make the proper connections. The speech therapist at the hospital had given us exercises to work on at home, and Joe diligently reminded me each day to do those with him. ("Name ten animals that begin with B." "Count backward from twenty to one", etc.) They were laborious for Joe, and he couldn't always finish them, but he pushed through his fatigue and did his best.

Once when we worked on saying our address, he did well repeating the house number; the street name and city took a bit longer, and "California" was just too much for that day. But he could say "this is weird!"

Fatigue had been an issue for Joe from the time he started on chemotherapy, but it continued even after he stopped the Temodar. He was still on anti-seizure medications as well as the steroid to reduce swelling in his brain. We found ourselves in a dilemma: too little steroid led to nausea and aphasia, but being on any amount of steroid equaled muscle weakness, extreme fatigue, and possible interference with certain chemo drugs that might be available to us.

The next few months brought good days and bad days. On good days Joe had an appetite and could eat normally. He could speak somewhat. Aphasia was a lingering menace but he could communicate, albeit haltingly and with much effort. He continued to practice playing the drums and to do household chores. He played cards with his sisters. He sometimes accompanied me on my errands to the grocery store and elsewhere around town. He took short walks.

On bad days he didn't have the energy to do any of those things. At times he was nauseated and couldn't eat much.

6/7/17
Lori

Joe has regained about 25% of his language skills and I am optimistic he will make a full recovery from the aphasia. Once again it's fascinating watching him try to regain his ability to communicate. Sometimes he'll want me to say a word, then he will work on saying it. At times his mouth does not cooperate and something different comes out when he tries to repeat the word.

He doesn't seem to have an appetite lately, and hasn't eaten more than two bites in a couple of days. Please pray for the complete return of his speech and his appetite. (He was visibly pleased when I told him I baked a chocolate cake today!)

His latest MRI shows definite swelling in the left frontal area (speech center), which Dr. Garcia thinks means the tumor "wants to grow". We have been holding it back with Temodar and Avastin for over two years, but they seem to have stopped working. Joe hasn't been on any treatment for several weeks (for various reasons). There are still other drugs we can explore.

We appreciate your continued prayers:

1. *for the swelling to decrease over the next couple of weeks*

2. *for no symptoms as he tapers off the steroid (usually headache, nausea, and speech problems)*

3. *for the return of his speech*

4. *for wisdom, courage, and peace all around*

   Thank you so much.

One afternoon when I was sitting in Joe's room with him, he opened the calendar app on his phone, pointed to a certain day and tried for almost five minutes to tell me something he obviously considered important. He kept repeating partial thoughts: "I couldn't…" "I wanted…" "I was trying…"

I made my best guesses: "You couldn't speak? You wanted to make an appointment? You were trying to write something?"

Finally he made a chomping motion with his mouth and put his hand around his throat.

"You couldn't swallow?"

"Yes!"

He was telling me he had trouble swallowing the day before.

I knew that was a bad sign, but I didn't want to acknowledge the seriousness of it, even to myself. Still, I told Joe we needed to let the doctor know at his next appointment. And I made a mental note to cook softer foods and pay more attention at mealtimes.

A few weeks later tumor activity once again necessitated a trip to the hospital—Joe developed severe nausea (this must have been so discouraging to a young man who really enjoyed food), and intense head pain.

7/18/17
Jeff

So we're still dealing with the latest bump in the road. By yesterday evening, Joe could not keep anything down, had a horrible headache, and the aphasia was maybe a little worse. Paged his primary Dr., who said take him to a local ER to get an IV in with fluids and the meds he couldn't keep down. They did a CT scan which revealed bleeding in the brain, and transported him to the UCI ER. Lori and I were with him there all night (Lori is still there). The good news is UCI said there is no bleeding. The suspicious areas were previous calcification (which they could clearly see with the benefit of prior scans). Joe is better, eating a bit, headache much less, aphasia about the same. They want to keep him overnight for observation and more tests, but so far no beds available, so he's still stuck in ER. Please pray that he'll continue to improve, and that we can get him on another cancer drug asap. Thanks!

After three hours in the local emergency room, then *twenty-four* hours in the crowded ER at UCI Medical Center, Joe was finally moved to a shared room around midnight. I went home to sleep for a few hours. I arrived in the morning to a loud commotion in his room.

"Get OUT! Get away from me! You're all FIRED! Get the #&%@ OUT!"

Joe's hospital roommate—we'll call him Fred—yelled profanities at the harried nurses and the young orderly assigned to serve him. I was told later that Fred had recently had brain surgery and was on a new medication; he was not himself. I was uneasy being only steps away from his unpredictability, but Joe seemed fine, and in fact whispered to me that we should pray for him, which we quietly did. Fred's wife and adult daughter stood huddled in the corner of the room and took it all in, confused and sad.

At one point Fred threw off his blankets and stormed toward the bathroom, shouting and cursing and "firing" people, his open gown useless in its intended purpose. He suddenly noticed Joe in the next bed and stopped.

"Oh! Hi—what are you in for?"

Joe was still having trouble communicating, but he was able to answer, "Mm, brain cancer."

Fred's face relaxed. "Oh man, I'm so sorry. That's terrible…I hope things work out for you."

He continued on to the bathroom, the nurse insisting that the orderly accompany him. Fred refused help and resumed his booming tirade, firing them both. Things got physical, security was called (a real cop showed up and was amazing in his ability to calm Fred), and Fred was moved to a single room.

A few minutes later, I ran into Fred's wife and daughter at the elevator. They were still shaken. They apologized profusely and insisted that Fred was a good man and they had never seen anything like this before, that they didn't even recognize him. My heart broke for them.

All this time, Joe seemed undisturbed. He expressed only compassion for Fred, even while Fred was making life extremely unpleasant for the rest of us. Perhaps he empathized with Fred's frustration at being dependent on others. It occurred to me later that Fred also felt compassion for Joe when he learned of Joe's cancer. Neither of them was in a position to offer practical help to the other. But I think in some odd way they may have connected in that brief encounter.

A few days later someone put me in touch with a clinical trial coordinator at City of Hope hospital in Southern California. They were running an immunotherapy trial that sounded promising, but Joe didn't qualify because he had a shunt. However, the coordinator was optimistic and said they were currently waiting for FDA approval for that very issue, and that she would let me know if anything changed in our favor.

7/20/17
Lori

Joe had several "sub-clinical" seizures (only observable on EEG) during his hospital stay so his anti-seizure meds have been increased. It would be GREAT if there were no further side effects as a result of the increased drugs. He was discharged last night and we got home around 8:00 p.m. Jeff brought dinner home from Rubio's and he and I ate and watched some of the Dodger game while Joe rested.

Joe was up and about for a few minutes today but is easily fatigued. Even so, he reminds me to do his speech/cognitive exercises with him daily. He eats small amounts of apple sauce and foods cut into very small pieces. I know that is a disappointment to him, and probably humbling, but he hasn't complained about it.

Thank you once again for your faithful prayers on Joe's behalf. Please be praying that he will stay otherwise healthy, build stamina, and that there will be no side effects from doubling his anti-seizure meds and the steroid. That's asking a lot, but God is omnipotent and gracious. He may say "yes". We of course are also praying for Joe's healing. This is a bold and audacious request, but I see no reason to stop.

However, God's ways are higher than ours, and we will love and trust Him regardless of our circumstances.

"The LORD will command His lovingkindness in the daytime; and His song will be with me in the night, a prayer to the God of my life." Psalm 42:8

Our house was disordered for a week while we had carpet torn out and hardwood flooring installed. We had to pack Joe's drum kit away in the garage during the renovation. Once we got everything back in place, it was great to hear him play the drums again—truly music to my ears. He gave me a drum lesson each week and I enjoyed practicing to the playlist he provided: mostly songs by Steven Curtis Chapman, Switchfoot, and Third Day.

In August we celebrated Joe's twenty-fourth birthday with his choice of pulled pork. I made (low-sugar) chocolate ice cream in the ice cream maker Joe had given me for Christmas the year before. It was a big hit—creamy and yummy. We sang our usual four-part-harmony rendition of "Happy Birthday" and relished each other's company. Food and music (and often laughter) generally happened when the five of us were together.

In the weeks that followed, Joe developed what his therapists called "foot drop": besides the partial numbness in his right foot, the toes on that foot dragged along the floor when he walked. He had to think hard about lifting his right knee higher than normal each time he took a step, so he wouldn't stumble. He was fitted for a foot orthotic (a specially-designed shoe insert), but it was uncomfortable for him so he didn't wear it.

At this time Joe was not on any cancer-fighting drugs, other than the twice-monthly Avastin infusion. His oncologists, Dr. Covachi and Dr. Garcia, had taken him off Temodar because it was no longer working. They wanted to try lapatinib, which had been used with some success against other cancers. But after several attempts by Joe's doctors to work with our insurance company, it was ultimately denied coverage. Several friends spoke with Jeff about the possibility of raising money to buy it outright, which we briefly considered.

Instead, we moved on to a different drug, etoposide, another which was being used against other cancers, but not glioblastoma. Joe took it for a couple of weeks and had such a bad time with it (severe nausea and weakness) that he decided not to continue.

When Joe admitted to me that he was beginning to get weary, I knew he meant something beyond physical tiredness. He was growing weary of the fight...

Around this time I had a dream about him. In my dream, three-year-old Joe came to my bedroom door as I was sitting at my desk. I went over to Jeff's nightstand to pick up a lime that had been promised to Joe, and found that it was brown on one side and mushy. I brought it to Joe anyway, knelt to his level, and tentatively offered it to him because I had nothing better. He looked sad and shook his head. I asked, "Are you sad because the lime is bad?" He nodded slightly.

I was filled with sadness and my eyes teared up. He seemed a bit confused and asked, "Why are *you* sad?" I answered, "I'm sad because my boy is sad." He seemed to ponder that for a minute, then I woke up.

I developed my own physical symptoms during this time. I often lay in bed at night and felt my heart racing or beating irregularly—it seemed to skip a beat then race to catch up. That made it difficult to sleep. I had occasional stomach aches and frequent headaches. Looking back later, I wondered if these might have been indications that I was beginning to grieve...

15

The Beast Advances

Though youths grow weary and tired,
and vigorous young men stumble badly,
yet those who wait for the LORD will gain new strength; they
will mount up with wings like eagles, they will run and not get tired,
they will walk and not become weary

—*Isaiah 40:30–31*

10/15/17
Jeff

First, thanks everyone for your continued prayers. Those who see Joe regularly have probably noticed he's not doing as well lately. He's lost almost all functionality in his right hand, and has significant difficulty communicating. His mind is all there, he's still sharp, but tumor growth is affecting the speech center of his brain resulting in a condition known as expressive aphasia. He knows the word he wants to say, but just can't make the connection to say it (or type it, or write it). Pretty frustrating, as you can imagine, especially for someone as articulate and expressive as Joe. And the last bit of bad news is that the chemo he was taking has caused him to lose most of his hair (again). But on the bright side, we were approved for a new treatment called Keytruda, which is an immunotherapy, rather than a chemotherapy. We're hoping to take the tumor by surprise. Would appreciate your prayers...

10/28/17
Lori

It is really hard for me to write updates these days . . .my tendency when things are bad is to hunker down and deal quietly with it. But as always, we desperately need and appreciate your prayer support. I know for sure that God hears the prayers of His own.

Joe had such a hard time on etoposide that he decided to stop it last week. He is still on Avastin infusions and has had one Keytruda infusion. Next infusions are scheduled for this coming Thursday, and he will decide next week whether to continue with those . . . He has been very nauseated for several days—not sure whether it is the tumor or the medications causing it. Jeff is taking him to the ER as I write (I am out of town for the weekend on a desperately-needed solo retreat).

While we appreciate the excellent care he receives at UCI, as you've heard me say before, hospitals are not conducive to rest and healing! So would you please be praying that God would settle his stomach today and that he would be able to come home soon?

Some of you will be thinking: try cannabis oil, drink kale juice, visit this doctor in this country . . . We are always researching complementary therapies, but the bottom line is that glioblastoma is a beast unlike any other. We do the best we can with what is available to us . . .

Joe's fatigue is severe and language extremely limited. As he has lost the use of his right hand and forearm, it is difficult for him to maneuver in his bed, so we are looking into renting a hospital bed. That saddens me.

He is so patient and never complains. He even asks how I am doing (migraines are back, after several years of relief). But he is so tired of fighting. When I mentioned the other night that I should update our Facebook prayer page, he weakly told me in broken sentences: "I don't want them to... pray for healing. I just... want to go home...." Since he was at home when he said this, he was, I assume, referring to heaven.

I have several requests for you prayer warriors:

1. *Relief from nausea; quick release from hospital (home is so much nicer)*

2. *Energy and peace for Jeff as he cares for Joe this weekend*

3. *Comfort and peace for Joe's sisters, Jamie and Anna. They have been wonderful, hanging out in Joe's room, singing, reading to him...*

4. *Wisdom and grace all around*

"Let me hear of Your unfailing love each morning, for I am trusting You. Show me where to walk, for I give myself to You." (Psalm 143:8)

After several hours in the ER, Joe was given another MRI which confirmed aggressive tumor growth—the beast had crossed the midline between the hemispheres of his brain. He was admitted to the Intensive Care Unit at the UCI Hospital. Jeff spent the morning with him and I arrived in the early afternoon from my retreat.

Jamie and Anna joined us a few hours later and brought takeout from BJ's restaurant so we could celebrate my birthday together in Joe's hospital room.

A nurse stopped the girls as they were coming in with the food to tell them it wasn't allowed, but reconsidered when she saw the looks on their faces. Two years later Jamie wrote the following reminiscence:

I'm sorry now that I don't remember your name. You were on shift that day in late October when my dad, my sister, and I joined my mom (who was nearly always there) in my brother's hospital room. Late October meant Mom's birthday, and we weren't about to let Joe's current hospitalization (ultimately, his last) hamper our celebration.

After discussing our options for a bit, we ordered online from the local BJ's, and my sister and I were dispatched to pick it up. I remember the way back being slightly confusing as we were on unfamiliar streets, and by the time we got back, heavy-laden, we were more than ready to eat and have a family birthday dinner—a Fischer family tradition as far back as I can recall.

As we approached Joe's door with the obnoxiously large and logo-plastered bags of food, you stopped us in the hallway. You said something like, "Oh, sorry guys, there's no outside food allowed. There's a risk of infection."

I honestly don't remember how we responded, probably something like, "Oh… really? We were just going to have dinner together…"

You stopped, considering the situation. I don't know what was going through your mind—maybe we looked particularly crestfallen—but you responded with, "Well… okay. Just keep it quiet."

That decision of yours was bigger than you'll ever know. That night we divvied our takeout feast out onto awkward paper plates and talked, laughed, and celebrated Mom. We took selfies together—at my demand and to Joe's chagrin—and these are the last family photos we have. Unbeknownst to any of us, that was the last family celebration we'd have together; I think it may even have been the last dinner as a fivesome (although Joe came home from that hospital stay, he was bedridden from that point).

So, I wanted to thank you. As I said, I don't know how you arrived at your decision to overlook the rule for us. Maybe it was just a snap decision. Maybe our faces changed your mind, or maybe you were just tired and this wasn't worth a potential argument. Or maybe you truly understood what was at stake. After all, you were his nurse and must have known the prognosis.

Whatever the reason, we're so grateful to you. You gave us so much more than just permission to eat our dinner. You gave us significant "lasts" we didn't know about, and you gave us memories that continue to carry us through our grief to this day. "Thank you" seems inadequate, but it's all I can think to say.

So thank you.

Sincerely,

Jamie and the Fischer crew

Joe spent the next four days in a regular room, then he was moved to the Acute Rehab Unit. The physical and occupational therapists were intent on helping him develop the skills needed to get by at home, such as helping us move him from a wheelchair to the bed, without him falling. He seemed to be getting weaker by the day and had almost lost the ability to walk. I spent my days with him and went home to sleep most nights, as there wasn't space for me to rest in his new room.

I didn't sleep well that week, and sometimes I would quietly get out of bed in the middle of the night, sit on the edge of the tub, and sob, my head in my hands. The thought of Joe dying was something none of us wanted to think about, let alone admit out loud.

There were a couple of bright spots during that week. Jamie and Anna visited him in the rehab hospital one afternoon; they sang together and joked as they usually did when they were together, and brought a smile to Joe's face. He couldn't talk much or sing along, but he was obviously cheered by their presence. He also had several visits from his friend and mentor Scott, who read to him and prayed for him. I know those visits were a comfort to him.

He spent almost a week in the Rehab Unit, but I could see he was fading fast. He was losing more of his words each day. He had very little appetite and was once again having trouble swallowing. He alternated between discouragement and apathy, and by the end of the week he was so weak he was unable to do the smallest of tasks.

One afternoon while Joe rested, Maria stopped by and the two of us walked to the Mexican restaurant across the street from the hospital for a bite to eat.

"How are you doing?"

"I'm actually feeling okay this afternoon. I should be really sad and stressed, but I'm not."

She was quiet for a moment, then softly said something that included the word "denial."

I pushed back immediately.

"What do you mean? I'm not in denial. I'm not denying anything—I am well aware of how bad things are right now. I'm not in denial…" (I used a lot of words to deny being in denial).

I don't remember her gracious response, but many weeks later I realized she probably meant I was denying myself permission to grieve, not denying reality. I knew in my intellect we were losing Joe, but my brain and my heart were not yet on the same page. When previously I had noticed my own physical symptoms of arrythmia and stomach aches, those were probably evidences of my withholding feeling grief fully. I think somewhere in my subconscious mind, grieving would have meant letting go. And I was not ready to let Joe go.

For reasons I still don't understand, the rehab team wanted him to stay another week, even though he was quickly declining and was unable to do any of the tasks they had for him.

After talking it over with Jeff on the phone, I sat on the edge of Joe's bed one morning and said, "The therapy here is great, but it doesn't seem to be helping you…"

He gazed up at me, his eyes pleading.

I continued, "Do you want to go home?" Relief washed over his face as he closed his eyes and nodded yes.

I called a meeting with the rehab team and sat down with about five staff members, including the director; I told them we greatly appreciated their time and their optimism, but we would be taking Joe home that day.

I knew he wouldn't be with us much longer, and I felt an urgency to get him home where he would be surrounded by people he loved and who loved him.

The rehab therapists were supportive and signed off on his discharge, giving me advice about which foods would be easiest for him to eat, etc.

Jeff met us at the hospital that afternoon, and after thanking the rehab staff again, we drove Joe home.

16

Home

For to me, to live is Christ and to die is gain. —*Philippians 1:21*

(Joe's favorite Bible verse)

11/10/17
Lori

I can already tell Joe is happy to be home and in his own bed. It is much quieter here, of course, and everything is familiar. Also it is generally a healthier environment. He has very little control over his body, so even turning over or sitting up is a big challenge. We need your fervent prayer support for this next phase of our journey: for grace, strength, insight, patience and good humor for all of us, and for Joe to start feeling better, both physically and emotionally. Thank you so much.

> *Though the fig tree should not blossom*
> *And there be no fruit on the vines,*
> *Though the yield of the olive should fail*
> *And the fields produce no food,*
> *Though the flock should be cut off from the fold*
> *And there be no cattle in the stalls,*
> *Yet I will exult in the LORD,*
> *I will rejoice in the God of my salvation.*
> *The Lord GOD is my strength,*
> *And He has made my feet like hinds' feet,*
> *And makes me walk on my high places. (Habakkuk 3:17–19)*

We found a wonderful hospice team who helped us care for Joe at home, and he was able to finally relax in his own room—no more needles, tests, or midnight interruptions. He seemed more at peace and less agitated once he came home.

He was still able to eat soft foods but didn't have an appetite. He slept much of the time.

But the most frustrating thing (for me at least): he could no longer communicate. I wanted to converse with him, to know how he was feeling about everything, what he was thinking. And, what he wanted from me. Was my presence in his room a nuisance? Did he want to be left alone? Or was he craving more attention, more affection? I made my best guesses based on the son I'd always known and the conversations we'd had since his diagnosis. I spent much time in the chair near his bed, sometimes reading a psalm aloud, sometimes reading silently or just thinking. At times I held his hand and spoke to him. And through it all, a constant stream of prayer weaving through the days.

Jeff, Jamie, and Anna each spent time alone with him as well. I was not privy to their words, but I know when either of the girls was with him, sometimes there was music.

Three pastors from our church also stopped by that week for a few minutes to visit with Joe and pray for him; we were grateful for their kindness and support.

11/15/17
Jeff

I think the analogy of an airliner is appropriate. For three years, we've been cruising at altitude; in the last few days, we've reached that point of the journey where we are preparing to land. We brought Joe home from the hospital last Friday. Since then, he's continued to lose physical capability on the right side, and can no longer walk. He's also losing more and more of his ability to communicate. He sleeps most of the day (and night), but does perk up when one or both of his sisters come in. And thankfully his appetite is back.

Lori and I met with his primary oncologist yesterday. We had already ruled out additional surgery, due to the poor risk vs. benefit outcome. We reviewed the latest MRI, and compared with one only a month older, we can see significant new growth in the tumor, with indications it is crossing the midbrain and headed toward the right side. We discussed the new medication

I mentioned earlier with Dr. Garcia as well. He was not super encouraging about the potential benefits, and it did come with some significant quality of life side effects. After a lot of prayer, and discussion with Joe, we've decided not to pursue that avenue either.

We shared with Joe the doctor's prognosis ("weeks, not months"). As he has been since his diagnosis, Joe is completely at peace with that. Much more so than Mom and Dad. We've signed up for hospice with a very highly recommended agency, and met with several of them today. Like I say, it definitely feels like we've begun the approach to landing, and all the changes in preparation for that are serving to make this very, very, real.

Throughout this journey, we have been sustained by your prayers. Can we ask you to please keep it up for this final stage? We don't know how long it will be. Joe beat the initial prognosis for someone in his condition by about double, so he may do the same now too. If so, this will be a long, slow approach, and we so need you all standing by us in prayer for the duration. Thanks.

11/16/17
Joe's friend Chrissy

Joe and Anna recorded this album a few years ago. I can't tell you how astounding the talent of this family is, especially Joe's in his musical ability, writing ability, and knack for mixing and editing. He also has a knack of being honest in the midst of pain, which he does on this album. Yet, along with being honest about his pain he also conveys his certainty in who God is. In conversation and in song Joe has always had this ability to be authentic about pain yet convey his complete trust in God. Additionally, this album is fantastic musically, all instruments played and edited by Joe. If you haven't bought this album, I can't recommend it enough. (She included a link to the album *New and Old*)

Chrissy visited Joe a few days after he arrived home from the hospital. She brought her guitar and sang to him and talked to him, although he could no longer respond. It must have painful for her to see one of her best friends fading away, especially since her beautiful mother had passed away of the same thing just three years earlier. But I have no doubt her presence was a comfort to Joe.

11/21/17
Jamie

Friends, I have a request. If you know Joe personally, would you share a favorite or funny memory you have of him? I love hearing them and I think it would provide a welcome little ray of sun in the middle of a difficult week for the five of us. Thanks in advance.

There were many, many responses to Jamie's request, and each one was read over and over by us and so appreciated. They were a great encouragement and a blessing to us. Following is a sample:

11/22/17
Scott Keuthen

I only came to meet Joe in the last couple of years. I was immediately struck by how simple and direct and unencumbered Joe's walk with the Lord is. I've always believed this, along with the sincerity of Joe's faith, has brought him great influence with many people. Joe is a remarkable young man. He's a pleasure to be with. His quick wit, wry smile, wonderful sense of humor no doubt gained from his family . . . of greater importance however, is his great conviction of the truth of Jesus Christ being alive and His salvation. I so love Joe's tender love for those who are less fortunate . . . the homeless, or anyone in need really. Since I've known Joe, he's been on the lookout for opportunities to serve others. This just seems right to Joe, like it's what he was always meant to do. Joe, you teach all of us to love others . . . to walk as Jesus walks by serving others. Joe Fischer, oh mighty man of God.

11/22/17
Cathy Plante

What an amazing young man you have there. My oldest son, Ethan, was part of the Friday group during his 8th grade year. Joe led worship back then and I had the privilege of hearing him a couple of times. I am incredibly sorry for what you're going through. Joe is an amazing child of God, serving the least of these even while he was sick. I wish this wasn't your reality, but please know what an impact you've made on me and all of us who read these updates. May God give you His comfort and strength.

11/23/17
Dan Weston (assistant Kajukenbo instructor)

When I think of Joe I think of a few different things. I think of how intelligent he is, how friendly, his sense of humor, and how intense he is. Kajukenbo is not an easy martial art to learn or train in. He had, from the very beginning when he was a little boy, such an intensity about him when it came to his focus on his training both mentally and physically. He became our youngest black belt ever at the age of 18, and those belts are not given away or sold, or awarded to children.

He was always somebody you had to watch when you were sparring with him no matter how much bigger you were than he was. If you let down your guard for a second, he would capitalize on that and be in there to tag you. It didn›t surprise me to find out that he also pursued his faith and his music, and his fight against this disease, with the same intensity that he brought to Kajukenbo, all the while retaining the Christian character that he brought to everything as well. I›m proud to know Joe and his family. They're some of the best examples of true Christianity I have ever seen. God bless!

11/23/17
Maureen Bosanko

There is a whole group of now 7th grade boys who would look forward to Joe leading worship at Friday School. In the homeschool world there are far more female role models than male role models at Friday School, and among the male role models, very fewer yet who are young enough for the boys to identify with. Joe was the male role model who taught them how to worship the Lord with their whole heart.

I remember once in Friday school the kids were chatting during worship time, and Joe, in his respectful, yet firm way, stopped worship and spoke to all of the kids about how this was their time to come before the Lord. The entire Friday school chapel changed from chatter to worship. I loved how he used chapel as an opportunity to teach the kids how to worship, not just to sing songs.

I know of at least 3 of these now 7th grade boys who have decided to play various instruments, Joe being an example to them since they were young that it is cool to be a guy and worship the Lord through music. One has already started leading others in worship like Joe. Thank you Joe for your dedication to the boys of Friday School. I'm sure you didn't know it, but through your consistent example at Friday School chapel, you mentored many kids in how to honor the Lord through worship.

11/23/17
Lori

Joe is not able to respond to us, not even with a blink or hand squeeze, but twice I have read some of your tributes to him and both times a tear rolled down his cheek. I am sure he had no idea how many people he has influenced for good—thank you so much for sharing. I imagine he is especially gratified to hear of the youth that he has impacted—he has always been kind of a natural mentor and is really good with kids.

And then there are the unseen ways he has served: the countless conversations with people living on the streets, and all the purchases of food, shoes, jackets, etc. for them. Serving at Food for Life when he barely had the energy to stand for an hour, buying a lawn mower so he could offer free lawn care in the neighborhood. Last summer he met a single mother in our neighborhood who was trying to get her house ready to sell. Joe walked up to her house every afternoon for several weeks to weed her garden in the hot sun. Anna or I usually went with him to help. He didn't feel great and didn't have a lot of energy, but he insisted on serving her daily. I realize I am gushing (and Joe would hate this), but there it is.

Thanks, Jamie, for the idea. And thank you all for providing some powerful encouragement for Joe in his last days . . .

Recently I saw a text exchange between Joe and the single mom mentioned above. In his text to her, Joe was apologizing to the woman for being "away for a few days." He didn't mention that he had just undergone brain surgery the week prior!

PART 2

17

Goodbye for Now

I have fought the good fight, I have finished the course,
I have kept the faith. —II Timothy 4:7

November 23, 2017. Joe is lying in his bed, his eyes closed, hanging on to this life by a thread. Jeff, Jamie, Anna and I sit with him. We sing hymns, the sun sets... moments later he is set free. He is carried home to Jesus, to the home he has been prepared for, the home he has been longing for.

Grief envelopes us, we move within its haze in the days and weeks that follow, bound together but separate. Jeff needs my companionship, I need solitude. In fact, I am desperate to be alone for months unending, to feel grief fully, to think my own thoughts without regard for anyone or anything else, but this is not possible. I have obligations, relational and otherwise.

Jeff has lost his only son. A boy on the verge of manhood, they were becoming friends. Jamie and Anna have lost a best friend and confidant. They have lost a music collaborator and a fellow jokester, the one who always laughed at their silliness and egged them on.

They each have their own story of loss and grief, of healing. I cannot tell their stories here; I cannot read their minds or see into their hearts. Their stories belong to them and they will steward them as they wish.

11/24/17
Lori

I shared with Joe a few weeks ago how he kind of reminded me of the character Frodo in Tolkien's Lord of the Rings. *He had this heavy burden to carry on a long and difficult journey, and although he was surrounded by friends, they could not help carry it—he had to do that himself. His friends could only walk beside him, protect him and minister to him along the way.*
Goodbye, dear Frodo. It was my honor to be your Sam.

I want so badly to just withdraw inside myself and not speak to anyone for many weeks. But there are details to attend to. Decisiveness has never been my strength, but now I must make one decision after another, and it is draining. I am slogging through mud, my feet heavy, my muscles weak, my mind fatigued and distracted.

Dazed and sad, I float through the motions of making arrangements, conversing with family and friends, doing errands, my head constantly buzzing. Jeff is busy, too, preparing for Joe's burial and memorial service as well as staying in touch with his work. He is experiencing double stress now: stress from work and the stress of losing his son. But he remains responsible and dependable even in his grief, and I love him for it. We lean on each other and help each other do each next thing.

We have a small graveside burial service on a brilliant autumn morning. Jeff's brother and sister-in-law Terry and Paula, along with their two adult daughters Holly and Hannah join us. Anna's boyfriend Elijah is there, so is Joe's friend Chrissy. Our pastor, Brian Benson, speaks words of comfort, then we sing "Amazing Grace". Joe used to play and sing that hymn often, so we feel it is fitting. We each drop a guitar pick on Joe's closed casket...

We make the serendipitous discovery that the burial site of Chrissy's mom—who died of brain cancer three years earlier—is about ten feet away from Joe's site.

The following week there is an afternoon memorial service at our church, attended by around two hundred fifty friends. Many people we haven't seen in a long time, or have never even met in person but who have been following Joe's story online come to show their support. It is a great comfort to have so many people come to remember and honor Joe, and to just be with us.

The passage we have printed on the back of the program reflects Joe's life: he did not fear when "the heat" of suffering came and continued a fruitful ministry until he was completely spent:

Blessed is the man who trusts in the LORD
And whose trust is the LORD.
"For he will be like a tree planted by the water,
That extends its roots by a stream
And will not fear when the heat comes;
But its leaves will be green,
And it will not be anxious in a year of drought
Nor cease to yield fruit. Jeremiah 17:7–8

The service is poignant and meaningful to us: Jeff has put together a video slide show of Joe growing up, with Joe's recording of his song "A Name for Me" playing. Our worship pastor Robbie leads us in singing Matt Redman's "Blessed Be Your Name". This lyric echoes Joe's attitude of accepting God's will and praising Him regardless of our circumstances. It says, in part:

Blessed be Your name
When the sun's shining down on me
When the world's all as it should be
Blessed be Your name

Blessed be Your name
On the road marked with suffering
Though there's pain in the offering
Blessed be Your name

You give and take away
You give and take away
My heart will choose to say
Lord, blessed be Your name
Matt Redman and Beth Redman
Copyright © 2002 Thankyou Music Ltd

Jamie, Anna, and Robbie sing Joe's song "Forward in the Darkness"— it is moving and I so appreciate that the girls are able to sing in the midst of their grief. Their voices blend beautifully, their harmonies perfect. Our friend Scott speaks, so does my brother Dave. Scott tells us that Joe was not just "an ordinary Joe". That his life's theme was putting the needs of others ahead of his own, his faith uncluttered by peripherals. That one of his most striking qualities was his influence, his leadership. He didn't look behind to see who was following him, but was always looking ahead to see who was in need. Scott said Joe once shared with him that he believed he was "supposed to be in this place" (having cancer) in order to help others somehow. Scott continued, "Today Joe is in glory, present with the Lord, out of reach of the gnarly grasp of the enemy... Joe taught us worship, humility, faithfulness, and joy."

Joe's uncle Dave shares many things about his impression of Joe, including the following: "Joe always took time for others. This became very clear to me during a family reunion trip to our family cabin in Lake Tahoe in 2011. During that trip, I would often see him sparring with my kids and his other cousins, who were also into the martial arts at the time, or taking long walks to the river with his sisters or cousins, or simply having long conversations with various family members. When Joe spent time with someone...anyone, I was always left with the impression that he wasn't hurrying through the moment. There was just a calmness about him and when you were with Joe, you had his undivided attention, even after the diagnosis."

Pastor Brian then takes us through stages of Joe's life using items I provide from home: the fedora Joe wore during his junior high years, his guitar, his hard-earned black belt, and his Bible. He emphasizes that Joe's life reminds us to use the gifts and talents we have been given to serve God by serving others.

We close with another Matt Redman song, "10,000 Reasons", whose final verse states:

> And on that day when my strength is failing
> The end draws near and my time has come
> Still, my soul will sing Your praise unending
> Ten thousand years and then forevermore
> *Jonas Myrin and Matt Redman*
> *Copyright © 2011 Thankyou Music Ltd (PRS)*

As we all stream out of the church building, we are greeted by a brilliant sunset, beams of light shining through clouds glowing pink and orange, a rare occurrence for the inland area of Southern California. Those who know Joe well know that he really appreciated a good sunset—is it possible God painted the sky so beautifully as a favor and a comfort to us?

We are also greeted by a massive dessert spread organized by the hospitality committee at our church. I so appreciate these behind-the-scenes people who are also detail-oriented. Jeff and I stand in the courtyard and greet our friends for over an hour. We are comforted by their presence, and I am grateful they have each made time to join us as we remember Joe's life and legacy.

Before Me

Before me I see a left and a right
And neither will advertise either as best.
However, I've certainly come here tonight
Not by the virtue of having guessed right.
I haven't guessed right but I'm right to have guessed.

Before me I see a city that glows
With patches of darkness between pins of light.
Behind I recall, as in its death-throes,
A sunset more brilliant than pins can compose.
And yet it gives way every day to the night.

© Joe Fischer 2013

During this time I meet—in person for the first time—Jill Crawley, a friend I have only known through social media. Our mutual friend Renee introduces us in the courtyard after Joe's service. Jill is an accomplished artist, and just a few weeks later, she gives me an invaluable gift, a painting she did from a photo of Joe. In the photo Joe is walking away from the camera on a lonely winding road in western Ireland. The photo is black and white, but in the painting Jill has added gold light spilling from around the bend, as if Joe is walking into heaven. It is a unique and thoughtful offering.

Our extended family and several friends join us at home after the service. My childhood friend Laurie has taken time off work and driven the four hundred miles to be here with us. There is food and we talk about Joe; Anna gets out her guitar (a gift from Joe) and we sing a few praise songs. I find that even though I often long to be alone, I am greatly comforted by the presence and care of people who love us. I will soon discover that I continually vacillate between the desire to retreat alone and the desire for close and meaningful fellowship. I guess I need both.

18

There is No Normal

When you pass through the waters, I will be with you;
And through the rivers, they will not overflow you.
When you walk through the fire, you will not be scorched,
Nor will the flame burn you.
For I am the LORD your God, The Holy One of Israel, your Savior . . .

—Isaiah 43:2–3a

I cannot fathom spending Christmas at home this year, just weeks after Joe has died. To try to maintain family traditions without Joe would only serve to make his absence unbearable. We discuss this as a family and agree that we will go away for Christmas. We decide on Palm Desert, a two-hour drive from our home. We stay at a nice hotel for three nights.

We all feel Joe's absence keenly, but in our sadness we find comfort in being together. Jeff reads aloud the story of the birth of Jesus from the second chapter of Luke; we must remind ourselves that Christmas isn't primarily about family—it is about God coming to us in the person of His Son, Jesus. We know that God loves us and has prepared an infinitely better life for us after this one.

Joe, too, believed there are much better things to come than what we see and experience in this life. He was living for that day—the day he would know and enjoy his Savior face-to-face. He made the most of his time here on earth, investing in people from all walks of life in many different ways. But he often felt out of place, like a visitor in a foreign land. Even as he gladly served others, he seemed untethered to this life.

"For our citizenship is in heaven, from which we eagerly wait for a Savior, the Lord Jesus Christ." (Philippians 3:20)

He had what my friend Sally called "a quiet inner stamina". The last several years of his life he was in and out of the hospital. He had his arm stuck with a needle almost weekly, he took powerful medications and tasteless supplements, his diet was sometimes restrictive, and he endured frequent nausea and increasing physical and cognitive limitations.

Yet he accepted his situation, pushed himself and got involved anyway. Whether creating music, mentoring, or feeding the hungry, he stayed engaged. How does a person walk that journey with such grace?

My best guess is that he chose to focus on the bigger picture:

"Set your mind on the things above, not on the things that are on earth." (Colossians 3:2)

Oh, Lord, help me to do the same.

It's always there, in the pit of my stomach. A dull ache that sometimes hides in the background of life, and sometimes clearly makes its presence known.

At times I'm barely aware of it. But then— I arrive home with groceries in the car and he isn't there to greet me in the driveway saying, "Mom, put that bag down. I'll get it". He doesn't show up at my bedroom door to hug me goodnight. Or Wednesday rolls around again and I am reminded I won't be driving him to UCI for his regular doctor visit. Or one of his songs comes up on my playlist and I realize he won't be sharing any new music with us.

I return to my part-time job teaching high-school Spanish for a large homeschool organization. I have thirty students across three levels this year. I love teaching these classes: the students engage well with the material, and we have a great rapport. When we resume classes after several weeks off for Joe's memorial service and the Christmas break, many of my students express their condolences, and I am touched by their compassion.

Some of them knew Joe, because they have grown up attending the Friday School Chapel hour, for which Joe led the worship music. This may be their first experience with death. They are mourning, too.

One of my freshman students, whom I've previously had to reprimand once or twice when his wisecracks threatened to derail my lesson, comes up to me my first day back, hugs me and says, "I'm so sorry for your loss." He never again is the class clown; he participates fully in class discussions, and I am proud of him. People aren't always what they seem. Or sometimes, they are one way and then they are another. We must let each other grow and change. I think he grew up a lot that year.

Somehow I am able to compartmentalize—I am fine while teaching my classes, but at home I wander through the days, restless and distractable. I cannot concentrate on anything, and I watch too much TV on my laptop in an effort to suppress the constant ache in my heart.

I reluctantly push myself out of bed each morning, make myself shower and dress, and attempt to attend to the business of maintaining a home, accompanied by an almost-constant low-grade headache.

While out doing errands I am hyper-aware of every irritation. It seems to me people are talking much too loudly, and the shrillness of their voices offends my ears. I feel raw and exposed, every nerve on edge. Strangers look right through me as if I am not there, or at least as if I don't matter. What is wrong with these people? Shouldn't they be grieving, too? For that matter, why are the stores and banks still open? Why are schools in session? Why does business continue as usual all around me? This seems wrong.

These days I can't abide small talk. It seems disrespectful to Joe, like his death doesn't matter and all is normal. Also, chitchat is just too much trouble—I don't have the energy. When store clerks innocently ask, "How's your day going?" or "Any special plans today?" I smile weakly while giving very short answers. Their questions feel like an invasion of my privacy; I do not want to chat. I'm afraid I may lack the appropriate filter—I may explain too much and make someone uncomfortable, or worse, say something unkind or offensive. So I try to be polite, say as little as possible, and hurry away.

Even when I run into someone I know, I still don't have the energy for idle conversation. I appreciate those who are brave enough to get right to the point, and sincerely ask how I am doing, even though I'm usually not sure how to answer. Socially I have conflicting desires, dueling voices in my head: "Please leave me alone" and "Please express compassion and show you care."

Most people I know are kind—they listen patiently when I go on about Joe and how much I miss him, and if they knew Joe they share their memories of him, stories I cherish. Some will text to let me know they are thinking of me or praying for me. They say, "Whenever you want to meet for coffee I am here." What a wonderful thing it is to be cared for.

In January I stay alone at a friend's beach house for four days. Jeff is kind to support my retreat—I know he doesn't like it when I'm gone. I walk the beach, read *A Grief Observed* by C.S. Lewis, and do a bit of writing. I assume I will use the opportunity to "process" my grief, but I don't feel much emotion. Am I numb? Or am I just doing surprisingly well this week? I really don't know.

One repeatedly piercing thought is that I wish I had been aware of the "last times". I wish I had known at the time: this is the last time we'll drive to UCI together (What would we have talked about? What music would we have listened to?). This is the last time we'll all eat together at the dinner table. This is the last time you will hug me goodnight, the last time you will speak to me…

Those last times just came and went without notice, because I didn't know they were last times. I want to go back and savor each one.

My daughter Anna is a singer-songwriter and poet, like her brother, and I love the way she expressed her thoughts on this subject:

> "but I don't remember the first times, and I don't remember the last times—I remember only the happy middle, when we were as much ourselves as we ever would be."

Our lives will never be the same. We are changed because we knew Joe. We are changed because we suffered with him. We are changed because we lost him.

Of course I am using "lost" metaphorically—we didn't misplace Joe. We know where he is. Jesus tells us, "I go to prepare a place for you" (John 14:2); he tells the repentant thief dying on the cross next to Him, "Today you will be with Me in Paradise" (Luke 23:43). I don't know exactly what Paradise is like, but I am confident it is wonderful and it is where Jesus is. Joe is fine.

The rest of us are gripping God's hand and trusting Him to lead us through this haze of sadness. It still does not feel normal to me. I'm not sure it ever will. I am eagerly anticipating the next life. Meanwhile, I believe the wisest thing I can do is stay near to God. Even when I don't sense His presence, I trust in His promises, such as, "He will cover you with His pinions, and under His wings you may seek refuge; His faithfulness is a shield and bulwark." (Psalm 91:4) and "He will wipe away every tear from their eyes;

and there will no longer be any death; there will no longer be any mourning, or crying, or pain; the first things have passed away." (Revelation 21:4)

I also find comfort in Romans 8:28: "For God causes all things to work together for good, to those who love Him and are the called according to His purpose." The implication to me is that God uses everything, even circumstances we would consider very bad, toward His good purpose, in the lives of those who love Him. I can't see a benefit to Joe's early death, but I choose to believe—even in the midst of great pain—that there is meaning in both his life and his death.

We all suffer to some degree. I see now that suffering is intrinsic to the human condition. Perhaps earlier generations knew this better than we do now. In former times, before Hollywood and Instagram and Madison Avenue tempted us with their collective mirage of perfection, I imagine our forebears knew early in life that there is no such thing as a perfect, trouble-free existence.

I cannot imagine going through such a painful time without the presence and comfort of Almighty God. I know God sees me, He cares, and He is using my suffering toward a good purpose. When I can't see the good purpose, all I can do is trust in His goodness.

19

Musings

My flesh and my heart may fail,
but God is the strength of my heart and my portion forever

—Psalm 73:26

August 28. Happy Birthday, sweet boy. (Sorry Joe, you'll always be my sweet boy). You would have been twenty-five today.

I miss you so much. I miss your dry humor, your wisdom, your practical help and courtesy, observing the friendship you shared with your sisters. I miss reading and discussing good books with you. Seeing your eyes light up when you spied a freshly-baked pie on the counter. Maybe most of all, I miss your music. You were a gifted songwriter, guitarist, and arranger. There won't be any new song reveals for us, not in this life. I am SO glad you recorded a few of your songs before you left us—I listen to them often, and they are a balm to my aching heart.

Tonight we will celebrate you, even though you are not here. We'll have one of your favorite meals: pulled pork sandwiches. And slaw, because veggies, and I'm mom. And peach pie. And we will talk and enjoy each other's company and share stories about you. Then we'll drive Jamie to the airport—where she will board a plane to begin her year-long Ireland adventure. She will be working toward her master's degree in English literature at University College in Cork. I know you would be so proud of her.

Happy Birthday once again, Buddy. I'm so thankful for the twenty-four years we had together. I am a better person because I knew you.

I take the tote bag out of the closet where it has been hanging for several months. It is a sturdy tote with "Alaska" printed all over it—I bought it on our trip to Alaska a few years back. It accompanied me to all of Joe's doctor visits and lab clinics, to the chemo infusion center and the rehab center, to emergency rooms and to the hospital for overnight stays.

I am not sure I am ready to face this, but I have put it off long enough. It has been seven months since its last use and it is time to clean it out. I pull out the black 3-ring binder that contains Joe's lab reports and monthly calendars of his appointments, printed out for me by the scheduling nurse at UCI. The last calendar page is August 2017—where is September? In September of last year we discovered further tumor progression and Joe had further symptoms because of it: increased aphasia, more numbness in his right hand, and impaired cognitive function. We were also trying to find an effective chemo drug, having exhausted all the usual options. Perhaps I was distracted and forgot to ask the nurse for a monthly printout.

Also in the tote are two business cards: one for Dr. Garcia—one of Joe's neuro-oncologists, and one for Dr. Garnier—the neuro-ophthalmologist who performed his eye surgery. There is a magazine for the times I waited for Joe to return from an MRI. A paperback Bible—Joe's eyes tired easily but sometimes he wanted me to read to him. And he always wanted to carry a Bible in case he had the opportunity to give it away. A deck of cards for passing the time together during infusions or hospital stays (we played Gin Rummy or Crazy Eights) whenever he was up to it, which wasn't often. He usually just wanted to rest. Water bottles, one for him and one for me.

Sometimes the tote carried snacks, but fortunately there is no forgotten food in it today.

Two pencils, a pen, and a blue composition notebook, in which I jotted down notes during doctor visits.

Pulling out each item brings unexpected stabs of pain, and tears fill my eyes once again. I thought I would just be cleaning out "stuff." But this tote bag was with us for all the unpleasant appointments and stressful hospital stays, so it also contains difficult memories. I am bombarded with recollections of all the suffering he went through. And, the suffering I went through watching him suffer.

Yet I am also reminded of how he did his best to make life easy for me: he never complained and tried to keep things light-hearted, in spite of how he was feeling.

I skim a few pages of the composition notebook. I stop and smile: among the notes about Joe's weekly weight changes and medication updates is a limerick Joe and I wrote one afternoon at the infusion center as he sat in the recliner, Avastin dripping into his vein.

> *There once was a nurse dressed in red*
> *Who treated the brain in Joe's head*
> *Stuck a tube in his arm*
> *He cheered her with charm:*
> *"Truly a smile's the best med!"*

(We couldn't think of a good last line, so this one was contributed by a member of our Facebook prayer group. I like it.).

The first time Jeff and I drove Joe to the doctor's office to meet with Dr. Garcia and learn about Joe's condition, we met a young man in the waiting area. He had cancer, too. He told us he lived alone and got himself to the clinic by taking the bus. He showed no signs of self-pity. Joe asked if we could pray for him and he gladly agreed, so we did.

This was the first of many times I felt thankful that Joe had a supportive and helpful family, and I was thankful too for the privilege of walking by his side on this journey.

It is about a year since Joe died. I am sometimes on the verge of tears for no apparent reason.

Memories of him flood my mind this week...

Homeschooling him—he struggled with spelling but excelled at thinking and problem solving (and art, music, economics). When he was four years old, I began teaching him to read; he quickly understood that letters have specific sounds, but he seemed both impatient and bored with the lessons. After a few sessions I looked at my sweet boy and said, "You know, there's no rush. You don't have to learn to read this year if you don't want to. Shall we put these books away for now?"

Visibly happy and relieved he replied, "Yeah, I think I would like that!" For the next several months I continued reading aloud to him (so did big sister Jamie), and once he discovered the Calvin and Hobbes cartoon books I left on the coffee table, he began reading them on his own, asking for help with an occasional word. From then on he loved books and was an excellent reader.

Teaching him a few guitar chords and watching him quickly pass me in ability, then begin teaching others.

Trips together—just the two of us: west Ireland, Lake Tahoe (with *two* flat tire adventures), Turlock to visit Grandpa and play and sing for him (even as my dad was beginning to lose his memory, he was so proud to show off his grandson to the residents at his senior center), Ethiopia with our church group with a two-day stop in London, where Joe became the self-appointed group herder—making sure he brought up the rear as we wandered the city so no one would be left behind.

Family road trips: even at a young age, so easy to travel with; the girls were, too. They didn't have "screens" then, but we did a lot of singing and listening to audio books. And magnetic chess. And when we tired of that, there were always windows to look out of. I think I passed on my day-dreaming talent.

Watching with joy as he became the youngest black belt recipient in his martial arts school at age eighteen, developing his gift for teaching as he coached the beginning students.

Sending him off on church group trips to Jamaica and Eastern Europe (later delighting in a private family listening party of his song, "Mission Trip Relationships").

The reward of hearing each new song he released.

Memories that bring both joy and pain…

Attending church each week strains my mood because I expect myself to be social and conversant. I love the Lord and I believe in the importance of meeting together with other believers on a regular basis. I know there is great benefit in worshiping with others who love God, holding each other accountable, and hearing the Bible taught by someone whose vocation it is to study it and preach it. I go because I believe it is the right thing to do. But still, it is hard for me.

I lack motivation to do much of anything creative, although I am learning to quilt by watching YouTube videos. I am very slow at it, but I enjoy the learning. I have purchased an inexpensive sewing machine and I find sewing quilt tops to be somewhat rewarding, although it seems I rip out seams more often than not. I do not yet enjoy the rest of the process: basting the top to the batting and backing (making the "sandwich"), sew-ing the three layers together (the actual quilting process), and adding the binding. But I will keep at it—maybe I will enjoy it more as I improve in my abilities.

I have started a blog (joefischermusic.com) based on Joe, his music, and my grief and healing process. I guess that counts as a creative endeavor.

Our dog Roxie, a friendly and smart spaniel mix we adopted from a shelter years ago, is my shadow these days. When I have been sitting at my desk for a couple of hours, she will come near and stand and look at me with her eyes sparkling and her tail wagging, and I can almost hear her say, "It's time to get up and move—let's go for a walk." I always comply because I know she is right.

Anna's little cat Cora has lost weight and is sneezing. Hopefully it's just a cold that will pass soon. I've started giving her fish oil and we'll add canned food to her kibble starting today, for the extra calories.

Jamie is living in Cork, Ireland for her graduate studies in English literature. Anna is living here with us and has two part-time jobs in food service. Jeff has been elected Vice Chairman of the elder board at our church, Chino Valley Community. He has much to offer in terms of intellect, creativity, problem-solving, communication, leadership skills, and so many other great qualities. He also sometimes teaches in our Sunday morning Adult Fellowship. He reads and studies the Bible daily, even taught himself enough Biblical Greek to be able to translate portions of the New Testament from its original language. I am glad he has opportunities to put his abilities to use in these ways.

Jeff and I both retired last year and we enjoy traveling and planning our next trips. Part of the appeal for me, I admit, is that it is an escape from the loneliness of being in the house without Joe. He lived in this house his whole life; his absence is conspicuous, sometimes over-powering.

For three and a half years my main role was as his caregiver, his advocate and companion. I attended virtually all of his doctor visits, lab visits, MRIs and other medical tests, was by his side when he assisted the less-fortunate (I see the irony—many would consider dying from glioblastoma rather unfortunate), helped with rehab exercises—physical, occupational, and speech—, read to him and played guitars with him, and generally enjoyed his company and friendship. He is gone now, and I still haven't found my daily purpose.

So it is a relief of sorts to get out of town, to be distracted by new places and experiences. I have always enjoyed travel, having visited many different countries over the years, in addition to driving all over the United States—with my parents and siblings when I was growing up, and with Jeff and my kids in more recent years. But I now have even more motivation to seek adventure beyond our community.

I have been reflecting on the events of the past year: In January of 2017 my dad died. I loved him very much and I miss him. All through 2017 Joe was in and out of the hospital, we were constantly chasing the perfect dosage and combination of medications and treatments; he endured aphasia and nausea off and on, and finally an unmistakable decline. In November of 2017, our wonderful son died.

A few months later, Jeff retired after over forty years of working full-time in the field of Information Technology. For the last sixteen years he had been a vice president in a large banking company, in a role he sometimes described as "herding cats," as it was his responsibility to make sure all the different departments coordinated and standardized their technology projects. His intellect and communications skills were integral to his success at work, but the job's demands wore on him. As soon as it was financially feasible, we agreed it was time for him to retire and invest his time and talents elsewhere.

Two months later I retired from teaching. I loved my role working with homeschooled high schoolers, but I was ready for a rest from the lesson-planning and homework-correcting, and I wanted to be available to travel more.

And although Jeff needs time to decompress from a stressful job, he has decisions to make about how best to spend his days, which are suddenly completely unstructured.

No wonder we sometimes feel we are reeling. The past eighteen months have brought much loss and incredible change.

And the trips we are planning won't really change that. Travel is an opportunity to experience variety in life, to see and learn new things about the world, to meet interesting people and eat different food, to get out of the routine. We certainly have many happy moments during our travels, and we bond over our shared adventures. But they do not erase our sorrow. We take our sadness with us wherever we go.

I miss my son every day. I miss his kindness and courtesy, his practical help, his humor, new song and poem reveals, his advice, his challenges (encouraging me to play the drums twenty minutes a day, or to make a timeline of my life—which I still haven't done; sorry, Joe), his interest in travel…

I would love to have known him as an adult, cancer-free. He was diagnosed at age twenty and died at the age of twenty-four. I will never see him make his way in the world and serve God through his personality and passions. I will not see him have his own place and be financially independent of us, making all his own decisions. I hadn't thought of it before, but this is one more thing I am grieving. I have had to let go of my dreams for his future.

I often think about what he would have become. I am sure his attitude toward the homeless would have matured into greater effectiveness and stewardship. If he'd found some very generous donors for The Statement, he would have been absorbed in bringing that dream to life.

And if that didn't pan out, he would have been working toward another career, maybe in music. Hopefully he would continue writing, recording, and releasing his songs, whether or not it was his career.

Perhaps his love of hiking would have led to week-long backpacking trips or rock-climbing adventures. Certainly he would have traveled more; he was adventurous and always open to experiencing new cultures.

He had started writing a science fiction novel: it would have been great to read that.

He was a natural teacher and counselor, and had an abundance of common sense, so more mentoring, no doubt.

I also like to imagine how he would set up his own place. I think he would have kept it pretty clean, with no clutter in the main areas. One room would be a music studio (maybe even the main room), maybe he'd have a small gym space to work out in. A small but well-equipped kitchen—he liked to cook.

More realistically, he probably wouldn't have been able to afford to live alone, not in Southern California anyway. So he might have had roommates. And if they were messy or loud, that would have been really difficult for him.

But what would he be like? What would my relationship with him look like? I am missing the opportunity to just be his friend. I am disappointed that he won't be around to help care for me as I age. He used to meet me in the driveway after I'd been out grocery shopping, insisting on carrying all the bags into the house himself, even when he was weak and tired from cancer medications. And I let him, admittedly because I was usually tired, too, and I appreciated the help. But also because he really wanted to. He liked serving people and lightening their load, literally in this case.

Several moms at church and in our homeschool organization have mentioned to me that they imagined their daughters marrying Joe, or someone like him. That knowledge comforts me, and I am thankful they share their thoughts with me.

There were a couple of girls he liked at different times during his teen years, and they inspired his best love songs. And I know there were girls who liked him. He didn't date much, though—he once told me he felt he didn't have much to offer yet. I know he was not a fan of casual dating—he didn't see the point. As for serious relationships, I think he feared someone might get hurt if things didn't work out, and he did not want to chance causing pain. I'm not sure he was aware that he was a hot commodity among the females in his peer group (or at least in the minds of their mothers!).

Hopefully he would eventually have met "the one" and most likely would have enjoyed a long friendship with her before falling in love. I can only speculate.

People talk about "beating cancer" or "losing his battle with cancer". I don't believe Joe lost a battle with cancer. He loved and served God and people to the end of his life. He won the victory in how he lived and died—with grace and strength of character.

I have fought the good fight, I have finished the course, I have kept the faith. (2 Timothy 4:7)

He didn't lose. He won, because he finished well. And I'm pretty sure he is still celebrating.

20

NYC

The LORD is close to the brokenhearted,
and saves those who are crushed in spirit.

—Psalm 34:18

I have always loved October. My birthday! Fall weather! But now it also holds the difficult memories of Joe's rapid decline the month before he died, when Jeff took him to the ER because of severe nausea. Aphasia was a problem again and getting worse each day. Joe spent the next two weeks in the hospital, declining steadily, until finally we told the hospital team we were taking him home. He could no longer walk or communicate. I noticed mental and emotional changes as well—he seemed to be fading away… We knew there was no more the doctors could offer him, as the tumor growth was out of control.

I could tell he was relieved to be home, where everything was familiar and there was quiet order. He seemed much more at peace in his own bed, surrounded by those who loved him most. We diffused essential oils, provided some of his favorite foods as long as he could eat, and read and sang to him.

My friend and neighbor Tami brought dinner over for us that week, including an apple pie baked specially for Joe. I was amused to see him push his dinner plate aside (laboriously—he was very weak) and his eyes light up when I brought it into his room. It was a wonderful gift from Tami for which I will always be grateful, especially because that was the last real food Joe ate. He began having more trouble swallowing soon after that and his appetite disappeared for good within the next few days.

Joe didn't seem "all there" the last week of his life. Although he was awake some of the time, he was not responsive, and it often seemed he was looking right through me. He couldn't help us when we turned him in his bed or got him up to sit in a chair. He didn't seem confused, he just seemed... absent. It was heartbreaking to witness.

One day I sat by his bed and read to him some of the many Facebook tributes people were writing about him. One after another, people shared how Joe had encouraged them or their children to deepen their faith, pursue their passion, or address their bad habits and be a better person. As I read these tributes to him, I saw a tear or two roll down his cheek.

So he wasn't absent after all.

Apparently he hadn't realized what a difference he had made.

Jamie is still living in Ireland but is planning to fly to New York City to be a part of the choir for Keith and Kristyn Getty's Christmas concert at Carnegie Hall. This will be her fourth time participating in this event. I am planning to join her there to spend some time with her for a couple of days, then attend the concert. I have never been to New York City and am looking forward to it. Mostly I am looking forward to seeing my daughter again—it's been several months since she moved across the Atlantic and I miss her.

We will fly home to Southern California together for her Christmas break. Jeff and I are taking the girls on a Christmas cruise to Mexico. Once again I don't want to celebrate Christmas at home—it would feel too sad and lonely without Joe. The girls have never been on a ship and we are all looking forward to the adventure.

Anna has asked several times these past few months if she can move into Joe's room and make it her room. I have been putting her off because I'm not sure I am ready for that change. We finally consented and she spent a couple of days moving her things. She is planning to go through Joe's unfinished music on his computer to see if she can complete and produce any of it.

It feels strange to me to have someone else occupying Joe's room. I said yes because it seemed important to Anna and she has been patient waiting for my answer. I couldn't articulate it at the time, but I feel like I didn't spend enough time in Joe's room when it was still "his", like I didn't say goodbye before things were changed.

But I am only thinking of myself. I have had over a year to do whatever I needed to do in his room. Anna is grieving, too, and perhaps being in her brother's room is part of her healing process...

I arrive at the hotel in New York City and am greeted by a jubilant Jamie running down the steps to greet me. What a welcome sight on this cold, blustery evening. We hug and chat as she helps with my luggage and settles me into our room. I spy a Nathan's hot dog cart from our high-rise window, and realize I haven't eaten in many hours, so I slip down to buy a sauerkraut hot dog. I am tired, hungry, and cold, and it is the perfect dinner for my first night in NYC.

This is a bittersweet experience. Jamie sang in this choir last year as well, and I had planned to join her then. I had my flight and hotel booked, and show tickets purchased. But Joe began declining rapidly in October, and I didn't want to leave him, even for a few days. I canceled everything. I couldn't have known—and didn't want to consider—that he would be gone before December even arrived.

So this trip brings back those difficult memories. But I am glad to be here with Jamie this year, experiencing New York City all lit up and decorated for Christmas. It is a curious state of being to feel both happy and sad simultaneously. I suspect I will always carry a measure of sorrow, even through the happy times.

Jamie has a choir rehearsal the next day so I am on my own. I walk through Central Park, watching squirrels scamper up and down trees. I wander around for a while near Times Square before settling in at a café with a bowl of hot turkey chili. Again, the perfect meal on a drizzly, windy day. I walk by Radio City Music Hall and decide on the spur of the moment to see the Rockettes. After walking for three hours in the cold, then standing in line for an hour, it feels so good to sit down, relax, and enjoy the show. The choreography is amazing and the dancers so skilled—great entertainment.

After resting in the hotel room I head back out to meet up with Jamie around nine p.m.; we join the Getty choir for their Christmas caroling stroll throughout the Midtown area. It is *so* cold but we are bundled up and it is fun to sing with others who love to celebrate the Christmas story.

We sleep late the next morning and share a corned beef hash plate for breakfast at the deli across the street. Tonight is the concert at Carnegie

Hall! Jamie will be in rehearsals all day so I decide to go the Museum of Modern Art since it is not far from our hotel and I can walk there. I am glad for the opportunity to view Van Gogh's *The Starry Night* and many other wonderful pieces, although the more abstract art is a puzzle to me.

MoMA's collection also includes pieces by Klimt, Klee, Chagall, and Picasso. I think Anna might appreciate these more than I do—hopefully we can take our trip here one of these years. She and I have been planning to visit New York City together for the past several years, but for one reason or another it has never worked out.

This evening I leave my hotel room and walk the few blocks to Carnegie Hall for the seven-thirty performance. It is a beautiful venue (although not the most comfortable seat I've ever known). The acoustics truly are excellent, and the Getty concert is fabulous.

Joe and I attended a Getty concert a few years ago and enjoyed the fun "Greengrass" music (their word for their unique blend of traditional Irish music and bluegrass). They are talented songwriters and employ world-class musicians in their band.

I think Joe admired the way they incorporate musical excellence and sincere worship, and I know he wanted to do the same. After several years of writing songs about the ups and downs of romantic relationships (and one moving song about the American Civil War), he wrote "Forward in the Darkness" and several other songs either about God or addressing Him.

I think given more time, he would have continued writing songs that honor God. Sadly, his mental sharpness began to decline just as his faith was maturing and becoming more focused and intense.

Perhaps he is creating those songs now.

Our flight home is not until later this afternoon, so Jamie and I stroll through an outdoor Christmas craft market at Bryant Park, then walk to the New York Public Library, not sure what to expect. We are amazed at how beautiful and ornate it is: marble staircase, richly-carved wood, fine art—it appears to be more of a research library and museum than a place to check out books to read for pleasure. Regardless, we both enjoy it very much.

Navigating two distinct seasons of life simultaneously is challenging: I am walking through a season of grieving and a season of learning to parent adult children. The latter is proving to be a difficult adjustment for me, probably compounded by my sadness and restlessness. I think I still have much wisdom to share but it is no longer my job to give unsolicited advice, nor is it always wanted. Stifling my opinions is frustrating and somewhat exhausting, like climbing uphill in mud. But millions of parents before me have made it through to the other side of this particular mountain; I'm sure I will, too.

I had a dream about Joe last night (same dream twice in one night). He was having vague symptoms but we didn't have a car available in order to go see a doctor. So he borrowed a bicycle and took off. When he returned I said, "Oh my gosh—did you ride that bike all the way to... Los Angeles??"

He smiled a little, slightly out of breath, and said, "Yeah. I needed to get checked out at the hospital." I think he also said something like, "They won't know anything for a while." He was tan and healthy and handsome.

Then he did the same thing again, or I had the same dream again right after that. It was good to see him, even if in a dream.

But it was unsettling. Why did I not take charge and help him in my dream? Why did I not take care of him?

I should probably see a therapist one of these days. I have heard about grief counseling, and I'm sure it can be beneficial. I suppose I just don't have the momentum to research finding a good therapist, then to pick up the phone and make an appointment. Then there's the cost. And what if I don't know what to say?

21

Remembering More Blessings

O my God, I cry by day, but You do not answer;
and by night, but I have no rest. Yet You are holy...

—Psalm 22:2-3

I belong to an online group for people who have lost family members to glioblastoma. As I read about the distress these people endured because of brain cancer, I am often struck by how comparatively easy we had it. I guess that's easy for me to say, I didn't suffer like Joe did. And no doubt he kept much of his discomfort to himself. But much of what I read regarding symptoms from treatment and from the cancer itself seem foreign to me.

Pain, for instance. Joe did have some monster headaches, but he never had what many call "cancer pain". His cancer originated in his brain and stayed in his brain. The rest of his body didn't always cooperate with him, but it didn't often hurt either, as far as I know.

Many caregivers describe major personality changes in their loved one, usually negative changes. Anger, anxiety, major depression, and fear are common. If Joe experienced those emotions he didn't share them with me.

Seizures, delirium, and severe confusion are mentioned as well. One man said his wife had nineteen seizures her first year after diagnosis and he didn't have a full night's sleep for over three years, always on alert in case she needed help during the night. Joe never had visible seizures; his seizure activity was only noticeable on an EEG test.

Long-term cognitive decline and even dementia are frequently noted. Joe's mental decline was noticeable to us mainly during his last few weeks. It was accompanied by aphasia (inability to communicate) so it was somewhat difficult to discern between the two. He did experience a constant "brain fog" throughout his journey and as I've already mentioned, he did his best to fight against it until the end.

Many also mention frequent infections such as cellulitis and bladder infections. Other than an early bout of pneumonia, I think the only infection Joe had was a case of shingles. He was generally healthy, even during typical cold and flu seasons. Before his last surgery in April of 2017, the resident doctor who looked over Joe's chart in pre-op told him, "other than cancer, you are a very healthy young man!"

As an aside, but worth mentioning: my own migraines virtually ceased during Joe's three-and-a-half-year cancer journey. What a blessing that was!

Caregivers use terms like "horror" and "nightmare" to describe their experience watching their loved one fade away as a result of glioblastoma. Several of them called 911 on numerous occasions when their family member fell and they couldn't help them up. Some of the caregivers are now suffering from PTSD or unrelenting guilt—even years later—over things they wish they had done differently.

I imagine many of them feel that God abandoned them when they needed Him. I know people who have walked away from their professed faith in God when a loved one died, adopting a belief that God is either evil, not so powerful after all, or simply doesn't exist.

It seems David of the Bible felt abandoned by God from time to time. But he also believed in God's goodness and had a solid assurance that God had not really forgotten him, that He was a faithful God. He wrote in the thirteenth psalm: "How long, O Lord? Will You forget me forever? How long will You hide Your face from me?" But only a few verses later he reminds himself and us: "But I have trusted in Your lovingkindness…I will sing to the Lord, because He has dealt bountifully with me."

The idea of being ignored by God or out from under His care is a chilling thought, and I want no part of that. I can't say our journey with cancer was pleasant, although we had countless pleasant moments. There were many setbacks and bumps in the road: Joe endured vision problems, nausea, headaches, constant fatigue, and several seasons of aphasia. He experienced feelings of restlessness and mild depression. And as his care-giver, it was hard to witness those things.

But I don't remember our journey as nightmarish or horrific. As a matter of fact, I experienced an inexplicable peace throughout those diffi-cult years. Even through the confusion and stress of those first excruciating weeks, when I couldn't *sense* God's presence or compassion, I knew He was with me. That assurance remains a treasure to me, because I have come to realize: I would rather be afflicted by God than abandoned by Him.

22

The Second Year

God is our refuge and strength, a very present help in trouble.
—Psalm 46:1

I've been thinking about the second year of grief. I've heard from many who have walked before me on this grief road that the second year is often harder than the first. I can understand that. For one thing, the first few months after your loved one dies you are kind of in shock and on autopilot. You can't believe this has really happened. Yes, the pain is acute and constant, and you miss him like crazy, but there is a part of you that is just numb. You see people going about their business and it feels surreal. Nothing feels normal.

Secondly, to be painfully honest, if you have been a caregiver watching your loved one suffer for several years, you are relieved that he is no longer suffering, but you are also relieved that the ordeal is over. Of course that comes with its associated guilt.

If you're lucky you have tons of support. Your friends check in with you often; even people you hardly know are sympathetic and concerned. People do things for you—bring you meals, send you cards. And that is as it should be. You need all the support you can get just to make it through that first year of loss. You need help even making decisions.

By the second year, everyone else has long since moved on with their lives. Again, this is as it should be; I am not complaining. But you don't hear his name mentioned nearly as often. And you hope people don't forget him...

You're also left with some of his things that you haven't been able to bring yourself to sort through, including things that should actually be thrown away, like his chemo medication. Maybe I keep it because his name is on the bottle. I fear that I may accidentally erase him from our home. So I keep things like that as a connection to him.

The other day I watched a TED talk about grief. The speaker had lost her husband in 2014 to brain cancer (GBM, same as Joe). In her informal survey of people experiencing grief, she found that the two most painful words people heard were "move on". Please don't tell your grieving friend to move on. One doesn't move on from grief, one moves forward with it. Joe will always be in our hearts and in that sense he is always with us. He is with us when we travel, when we eat, when we sleep, when we laugh, when we attend church or a concert. He is even involved in some of my decision-making, as when I ask myself, "What would Joe say?" or "What would Joe do?" He has influenced me and is a part of me.

I'm not sure I've moved forward yet, but I can see that happening in the foreseeable future. And I am fortunate to have friends who do check in to ask how I'm doing, and who continue to share their Joe stories with me. My friend Renee is extremely busy with work, travel, and family life, but when we get together every few months, she is entirely engaged in the conversation and never in a hurry. She took guitar lessons from Joe and misses him, too. Michelle and Jan and Karen didn't know Joe very well, but they know and care about me, and continue to check in regularly. I always enjoy my time with each of them. My friend Joanne took all of the tributes to Joe from our Facebook group page and put them in a book for me—a priceless gift. My long-time friend Maria (almost four decades now!) and I get together often. I communicate frequently with my brother and sister. My neighbors, siblings, and other friends from church mention Joe without awkwardness, and I appreciate their thoughtfulness in remembering him to me.

I have met people who seem joyful all the time. I admire them but don't understand them. Surely these people have faced adversity, too. Is it possible they have learned the secret I am just beginning to consider: that joy and sorrow can walk hand in hand?

Early spring…it is cool and sunny most days, with occasional rain. Trees and bushes are budding, my roses are waking up and beginning to sprout leaves again. The hills are vivid green and I have seen a few calves among the cows on the hills while driving to town. This is a beautiful time of year in our little Southern California community. I get outside and walk every day, sometimes finding myself at a nearby park. There is something so restorative about nature.

Joe and I often walked up to the park during his last few years. We would sit on a bench and talk, or just enjoy listening to the birds. He sometimes brought his guitar (and insisted on carrying it himself).

Our last visit to a park together was in September of 2017, just two months before he left us. We drove a few minutes to Carbon Canyon Regional park, then walked a trail that led back behind the main park to a small secluded redwood grove. What is usually a ten-minute walk became a forty-minute walk as Joe had to walk slowly and carefully on the rock-strewn path, so as not to stumble or fall. Maybe not my best idea, this park. It was hot that day, and it was almost too much for him. But the grove rewarded us with its own cool, shady microclimate, and we rested there and enjoyed the silence before heading back to the car.

Oh, Joe, I miss you so much.

Anna has moved to Simi Valley (ninety minutes north) to begin a job in radio production. She has audio engineering skills and will be editing sermons for Christian radio. I know she misses her brother greatly—they were good friends and they share some personality traits: introspective and intellectual, with an endearing understated humor; both of them poets and songwriters.

Recently I began going through Joe's room. I am saving some things and having a quilt made from some of his shirts. I can almost hear him: "Mom, really? A quilt? Somebody could be wearing those shirts."

And I reply: "I *am* giving away most of your clothes. I'm sure someone will benefit from your pants and shoes, and your robe and slippers." And then my voice begins to crack with emotion: "I have to save a few things. You're not a mom, so I don't expect you to understand. It's just the way it is."

And he replies with a shrug, "fair enough" or "cool beans" and I continue my work.

I bury my face in his lined denim jacket and inhale deeply. It makes me miss him more but I can't help myself. Everyone has a scent; Joe's was mild and masculine at the same time. I claim his red and gray zippered hoodie jacket for myself. I will wear it around the house on chilly days, and sometimes when I go out walking.

There really isn't all that much to go through—Joe was not a hoarder. In fact, early in 2014—just months before his diagnosis—he did a major clean-out of his room. Seemingly out of the blue, he just decided one week to get rid of everything that wasn't necessary. He wasn't very attached to "stuff", so he basically went minimalist. I actually had to retrieve a couple of things from the give-away bag because *I* didn't want to part with them.

I wonder why he did that—get rid of his things, at that time.

Just a coincidence? Or—do people really have premonitions? Is it possible he had a hunch he wouldn't be around much longer, even before he experienced symptoms? And how long did he have symptoms before he mentioned them?

He had a stoic personality; it's not a big leap to imagine he may have kept some things to himself before admitting he needed help. I don't think I ever thought to ask, "When did you *first* notice you were losing peripheral vision?" "When did your headaches return?" "Did you have queasy days before you finally called in sick to work?"

On the other hand, I know his doctors asked him similar questions and many more. I'm sure they carefully constructed a timeline based on his answers. So once again, it appears my mind is wandering and creating unnecessary guilt.

Even though there's not a lot of stuff, it is taking me a long time. There are items in addition to clothes to sort through. At times I come across something that especially captures my attention... a scrap of paper with the start of a poem (for a man who didn't talk much, he sure had a way with words), or notes from his martial arts training. The journal he kept during a trip to eastern Europe. I can only manage about twenty minutes at a time before I feel the need to stop for the day and think about something else.

There was a potted tree in Joe's bedroom for many years, and it flourished there by a sunny window.

Early in 2014—around the time of his big clean-out, he cut it way back. He basically cut the tree down, leaving only a stick in the dirt. I was dismayed, but kept my emotions in check while I asked him why he did it. (What I thought: "What on EARTH were you thinking? Why would you destroy this perfectly beautiful tree?!" What I actually said: "So why'd you cut it back?").

His answer: "I just wanted to see if it would grow again."

He moved it outside and continued to water it.

A few months later Joe was diagnosed with brain cancer. We more or less forgot about the tree for a few months while we adjusted to a new routine. Later that year, we noticed the "stick" was taller and seemed to be turning green. Early the following spring—sure enough—a couple of leaves sprouted from the stick. Joe began to water it again and cared for it throughout his cancer journey. Every few months it grew another layer of leaves.

It is beautiful and lush once again, but it seems to have stopped growing—it probably needs a bigger pot. I can't help thinking that it kind of parallels Joe's journey: cut back severely, it remained alive and growing for three years before resting.

A Reason

Is there a reason that the wind
Should pick off leaves and bring them in
To my garage, where they begin
To beautify the mess within?

Is there a reason trees should bring
In birds to trade their leaves for wings?
The tree that gave me everything
Will still be clothed, and now it sings.

Is there a reason things the size
Of cities dominate the skies
Instead of falling down, capsized?
Is there a reason water flies?

Is there a reason clouds should hate
Their hue enough to confiscate
The waves that, when they radiate
At light speed come eight minutes late

And with them change their color scheme
To something out of someone's dream?
How much more content they seem
To blush than block the final beam.

Is anybody looking west
To see the sunset at its best?
I fear that I may have confessed
Too little of my love to rest.

© Joe Fischer

23

Music . . . and Another Christmas

Sing to the LORD a new song...
—Psalm 96:1

Jamie is back from her year abroad. She will return to Ireland in a few months for her conferring (graduation) ceremony to accept her Master's Degree. She loved Ireland and made good friends there. But she is glad to be home. And we are glad to have her back, after a whole year away. Her easy, happy nature is a balm to us. Jamie, who at age three made baby Joe chortle with glee as she rolled him across the floor. Who clapped and cheered when he first crawled. Who from around ages seven to twelve directed and produced the many variety shows she and her siblings put on for Jeff and me, telling them where to stand, what to sing, and when to exit the living room and hide behind the sofa, "off-stage."

She loves having the family together, and when she is near I am inspired not to brood too much. She lives nearby, sharing an apartment with a friend, and treasures her job at church, as the assistant to our worship pastor Robbie. She sings on the worship team most Sundays.

August 28. Another birthday for Joe…he would be twenty-six. These special days may get easier with time, but for now they still bring a tinge of sadness, and this year, nostalgia. For some reason this week I am thinking of Joe's early days, when "yoo-ya" meant "hallelujah" and "bop" meant "stop". Big sister Jamie was "Mimi". And one of my favorites was "howp-tah" (helicopter).

August 28, 2019
Facebook post: Chrissy

Today is Joe's birthday.

In recent months, I nostalgically listen to Switchfoot and enjoy re-membering all the times we goofed off at rehearsals playing songs from their earlier albums (strictly- I wish I could know what Joe would think of their new music). I listen to hymns and think fondly of when we lost track of time playing their choruses again and again (once, he changed the key 5 times in a song during rehearsal. Ironically, the song was "I Could Sing of Your Love Forever...").

But nothing is quite like his own music, his own gift we get to listen to. "Don't Feel Like Moving On" and "Lockpicks" are my personal favorites of his.

Happy birthday to one of the best friends I could have ever asked for. I'm grateful that we can still hear and celebrate Joe through his music.

"As for fear, I said so long . . ."

I like those two songs, too. When I first heard "Lockpicks" I said, "Joe! When did you learn to play piano?!" I hadn't heard him play the piano since he was about nine years old.

He replied matter-of-factly, "Last night."

He had taught himself just enough piano to get the riff he wanted for that particular song. He recorded it on our hundred-year-old upright, and the old-timey sound is perfect for "Lockpicks."

When he was around three years old, Joe liked to sit and "play" the piano. He couldn't actually play any songs at that age but he had a nice touch and it was pleasant to listen to. Here's an entry from the journal I kept for him during his childhood: *Yesterday after tinkling around on the piano for a minute, you announced that now you would play "Jesus Loves Me". You played a few notes, then stopped—obviously disturbed—and asked with fur-rowed brow, "why doesn't it sound like 'Jesus Loves Me'?"*

When he was six, he was cast in a school musical and had a solo. He did a great job—right on pitch, perfect tempo. He told me years later that if he'd known it was allowed, he would have declined that role. He didn't real-ize he'd had a choice. He did not enjoy being the center of attention. Which is a bit ironic, since in later life he often found himself in leadership roles, especially in regards to music.

Fortunately he eventually learned to handle attention with grace and good humor.

Joe had a fun creative streak and often recorded unusual sounds to use in his music. He called it sampling. I recall one afternoon I came downstairs to find him standing at the dining room table carefully filling wine glasses with varying levels of water.

He dipped his finger in water and ran it around the rim of each glass to hear the note that played. (I may or may not have done this with my friends at wedding receptions when I was in college).

He had his electronic tuner nearby and he continually adjusted the musical pitch of each glass by adding to or reducing the amount of water until he had it just the way he wanted it.

He then recorded the sounds as he played each glass. He used this feature in the chorus of his song "Don't Feel Like Moving On".

The holiday season is coming up, our third Christmas without Joe, and I still am not ready to celebrate at home. The holidays are especially difficult because Joe died on Thanksgiving Day. I begin to notice the ache in my heart, even after months of normalcy.

I visited Joe's gravesite recently. It was cool and sunny and there were very few people in sight. I sat and listened to the birds singing and the trees rustling in the breeze. A hawk circled overhead and a black phoebe landed nearby. It was actually pleasant. I know Joe is not there—his spirit is in heaven (I wonder: does he remember me?). But sitting up on that quiet hill is a comfort; it provides a focused time to remember Joe, and there is healing in those moments.

Once again I don't have the emotional energy to decorate the house or plan a special meal, so we plan to go away again for Christmas, this time to Laguna Beach. Jamie, for whom traditions bring great meaning and comfort, does talk us into getting a Christmas tree.

She has just started dating Peter; it is Christmastime and she is in love. He is smart, mature, and I like him already. She and Peter and Anna go out to buy a tree; they set it up and decorate it. She has a few friends over to watch *White Christmas*.

My family is so accommodating to me; I need to remind myself that I am not the only one here who is grieving and it is different for each of us. Jamie needs to maintain traditions; I need to do something completely different. Jeff needs togetherness, I need solitude. Anna needs routine but loves variety. We are all seeking balance in our relationships and activities. I sense God's Spirit working among us, helping us all to be gracious and understanding toward each other. We find ways to compromise.

24

Depression

He who dwells in the shelter of the Most High
will abide in the shadow of the Almighty.

—*Psalm 91:1*

We decide to cancel our Laguna Beach Christmas plans: the girls have work commitments on Christmas Eve so we wouldn't get there until very late at night. Rain is forecast, and traffic will probably be terrible. We decide at the last minute just to stay home. Christmas is two days away and I haven't made any plans. This will be our first Christmas at home since Joe died, and I am not ready.

Peter's mother Diana has come to the rescue. She has invited us all over for Christmas dinner and Jamie is so excited to introduce the two families. I am both impressed and truly grateful for Diana's hospitality—to include four extra people (three that she's never met) to her already-full Christmas table is beyond generous.

As it happens, Christmas Day is pleasant—just a quiet morning at home for the four of us. We exchange a few gifts and have a delicious break-fast—Jamie bakes caramel-pecan rolls and Anna whips up an egg-spinach-mushroom scramble. I am so grateful for their help; although I function fine throughout the year, I still don't have the energy to "do" Christmas, at least not in the same way as in the past. We light our Christmas candles while Jeff reads from John 1 and Isaiah 53, and we contemplate the incredible gift of God's Son, who came to show us who God is. I am reminded once again: Jesus understands our suffering.

We rest for a while, then dress and go to Diana's to meet Peter's family, including aunts, uncles and cousins. They are all friendly and likeable, and we are glad to have made these new friends.

It is spring of 2020. Jeff and I were scheduled to leave on a cruise to Hawaii with my sister and brother-in-law this week, but the cruise has been cancelled because of the coronavirus pandemic. It is a depressing and confusing time throughout the world. Schools are closed, restaurants are closed, even the churches are closed for the time being, although our church and many others will be livestreaming the music and sermon so we can watch at home.

Grocery shopping is an eerie and unproductive experience. People are buying up and hoarding supplies and most of our local stores have many empty shelves (toilet paper and bottled water seem to be especially popular—I'm not sure why. Are people afraid the virus will cause plumbing systems to fail?). I see fear in the eyes of strangers, the eyes being the only part of their faces that are visible above the face masks we have all been commanded to wear while out in public. Irritability and frustration are in the air, compounded by uncertainty—when will this end?

My sweet dog Roxie has declined sharply these past few weeks—arthritis is taking over. She stumbles sometimes and is often incontinent, but she still "asks" me to take her out front every afternoon. Only now instead of going for a walk she is content to lie in the sun while I sit on the porch and keep her company. I am heartsick… she has been my constant companion for twelve years and was by Joe's side during much of his decline. She has been such a comfort to me during our difficult journey. I will miss her terribly.

I go walking each morning; the weather is gorgeous now, cool and sunny. I still feel weak and tired most of the time, and each morning I wake up groggy, not refreshed. I try to walk one mile each day, but I walk slowly and I stop to rest at the benches along the way. I am chronically fatigued but Chronic Fatigue Syndrome has been ruled out by my doctor. Jeff says maybe I need more iron, but surely that would have shown up on my recent lab work. Also I've been tested for anemia before and the results were normal.

I was born and raised in California and have never lived anywhere else. I keep thinking I want to move to another state, just for some variety, for the adventure, to jog loose the parts of me that are stuck. But Jeff loves the weather here (and I must admit, it's pretty perfect), and of course our girls are here. So we stay.

I am often restless, bored and unmotivated. I have plenty to do and I keep busy with menu planning, shopping, cooking, cleaning and organizing, reading, doing my Bible study homework (and attending our weekly Zoom meetings—the pandemic precludes us meeting in person), and I've just begun reviewing my Latin materials—I taught myself a bit of Latin a few years ago and would like to pursue it further. I write blog posts and have started writing this book, although I find I cannot write much at home—I have to take myself to a local coffee house in order to be productive. I am as busy as I want or need to be. So when I say I am bored, I don't mean I have nothing to do. I mean I lack focus and nothing seems interesting for long.

My self-diagnosis? Mild depression.

I have had depression before, and I recognize it. My mom died of Multiple Sclerosis complications when I was thirty years old. I spent the following year in a depressive slump. I wasn't employed at the time and didn't yet have children, so I had a lot of free time. Even so, I could not bring myself to be very productive—I did the minimum of housecleaning and shopping. Mostly I sat in silence at home or went to the movies by myself during the day, while Jeff was at work. I had trouble sleeping and quite often took walks around the neighborhood in the middle of the night. Or I would get up and pace around the house for two or three hours before going back to bed, exhausted but not relaxed. Eventually the black cloud lifted and I began to feel normal again.

The next time I experienced depression was a few years later during my homeschool career. This time I put myself under a doctor's care and took medication for two years, which helped to stabilize my mood. I also reluctantly took a one-year break from homeschooling. After about two years, with my doctor's permission I weaned myself off the drug and found I no longer needed it.

So I could go back to the doctor and probably get medication again, but I don't want to do that just now; I don't want my emotions dulled. I want to feel my grief fully. What I am experiencing now is a much milder version of what I felt in the past. Although I am often sad and restless, I can function fine—I'm not curled up in a ball or refusing to get out of bed.

I'm not taking midnight walks alone. I am eating well and exercising. I am fairly certain I will know if and when I need professional help; and if I don't recognize the need, I'm sure my husband will let me know.

Obviously this is my experience only. If you are depressed, please tell someone, preferably a doctor. Do not suffer alone.

25

Guilt, More Loss, and Travel during a Pandemic

You have grief now, but I will see you again,
and your heart will rejoice,
and no one will take your joy away from you.

—John 16:22

Both girls have moved back in with us temporarily and are working from home. Their places of business are closed because of the pandemic, and we have Joe's recording and audio equipment that Jamie can use for her job as our music pastor's assistant. We all like living together again. (I just have to try not to care too much about the extra clutter—it can easily make me edgy if I let it). With the girls living at home again we are having Saturday Family Nights. Last night we played Hearts (Jeff's choice). I was winning until Jeff "shot the moon" and pulled ahead of everyone to win. Respect.

It is Mother's Day 2020. After online church (we are still not allowed to meet in large groups, per federal mandate), Jamie and Anna made a delicious lunch for us: broiled salmon, linguine w/ mushrooms and tomatoes, steamed broccoli, and strawberry shortcake. Everything was great and it was such a treat to have someone else do the cooking. Then they gave me a spa day in my bedroom: manicure, pedicure, facial, and scalp massage. They had pleasant music playing, candles, tea, flowers… they put a lot of thought into creating a lovely and relaxing atmosphere. Dear Jeff was left with a really messy kitchen to clean up on his own…another much-appreciated gift!

I have discovered to my surprise that I don't have nearly as hard a time dealing with Mother's Day as I do with the fall and winter holidays. I become more pensive and sad around early November...

Jeff is still serving in a leadership role at church and there are so many decisions facing the staff and lay leadership regarding this COVID-19 shutdown. How soon can we begin meeting together again? Would we be able to maintain a proper distance between family groups? Would it be possible to meet outdoors, and if so, what are the ramifications of that in terms of sound equipment, shade from the sun, etc.? Will we require masks to be worn, or leave it up to individuals?

By the governor's order, we are still not permitted to meet together in large groups. Our church leadership wants to obey the law (Romans 13:1–5) while providing meaningful worship services that honor the spirit of "let us not neglect assembling together" (Hebrews 10:25).

Jeff is well-equipped to serve on the elder board. He is smart, articulate, and ethical. I am proud of him. He continues to teach on occasion in one of the Adult Fellowships on Sunday mornings, and he and I teach the New Members class at church.

Jeff has also begun teaching himself a programming language that will allow him to develop apps for his smart phone. He does it to keep his mind active and challenged. I am glad he is finding his footing in this season of retirement. When he really wants to relax, he watches sailing videos on YouTube and dreams of selling the house, buying a boat, and sailing around the Caribbean indefinitely. I am not keen on this idea. I love to travel, but I need a place to come home to.

Today after a routine visit with my headache doctor, I was remembering Joe's migraines as a child. He would frequently get them Sundays after church (sensory overload, fatigue, hunger—a perfect storm, poor little guy). Typically he would throw up, then I would put him in the car and drive around the neighborhood for thirty minutes or so until he fell asleep. He told me the movement of the car made him feel better. When he awoke later he would be fine.

I feel so guilty for putting him through the stress of several hours of Sunday School every week. Maybe we should have cut ourselves back to one service, or at least had him sit with us during either our Adult Fellowship hour or the church service—either would have certainly been less noisy and chaotic than second-grade Sunday School all morning. As a fellow introvert I can certainly relate to the social exhaustion.

But now that I think about it, I recall he did sit with us sometimes. In fact we often gave him the choice: attend his own Sunday School class or sit with us in ours. It's possible some of my guilt is misplaced. I do have a habit of only remembering negative things—why do I do that?

He did grow out of the chronic migraines, just as our pediatrician said he would. Naturally when I began thinking about this, I ran to the internet to research. Thankfully, the consensus is that childhood migraines do not cause brain cancer.

Our little cat Cora died recently. One day when she didn't come into the kitchen for her breakfast, we found her lifeless under the sofa. A few weeks later, we said our goodbyes to Roxie, our dog. The veterinarian told us that by the looks of her X-rays, she'd most likely been in considerable pain for a long time. She had seemed happy to us—even as she stumbled while following me from one room to another she would be wagging her tail and showing her same happy expression. He said dogs are stoic that way and are good at hiding their pain. Both Jeff and I were with her at the end.

Interesting that we—people in general, I mean—put ourselves through this. We know full well we will probably not outlive our pets. Clearly those of us who keep pets feel that giving them a loving home and enjoying their company for a few years is worth the pain of losing them. But it is so hard to say goodbye…

So we are currently petless, for the first time in our marriage. I think we may keep it this way for the time being. Our many pets have added affection and energy to our family life over the years, but both Jeff and I kind of want a break from the responsibility for a while. We also intend to travel more—once the pandemic is under control and travel restrictions ease—and it will be nice not to have to make arrangements for pet care while we are away. I'm sure eventually we will adopt another furry friend.

I still haven't finished going through Joe's things. There are a couple of dresser drawers that hold some clothes and a few other items. Again, there's not much there, but for some reason it's just hard to face the finality of what the task represents. So I allow my days to fill up with other activities…

Jeff and I attended my nephew Tim's wedding in Modesto this weekend and are taking a road trip back down the California coast. I have always enjoyed this drive, but traveling isn't as much fun as it used to be because of the COVID-19 regulations and limitations: most restaurants are closed and businesses require us to wear masks. Carmel is especially stringent, only letting one or two people at a time into shops, and requiring masks even outdoors when no one else is near. Between that and the persistent fog, we are ready to move on after two days. We do enjoy a walk on the trails in Point Lobos State Nature Reserve for a couple of hours—it is cool and misty but still beautiful. We can hear sea lions when we get near the ocean but can't see any as visibility is low.

We check out of our hotel and drive to Big Sur for lunch. I have been here when it is breathtakingly gorgeous, but today the fog hides the ocean. I generally enjoy cool gray days at home, but this part of California is known for its dazzling views of the ocean and the beautiful state parks, so we are a bit let down. (Admittedly, this area is also known for foggy mornings).

Cambria, however, is sunny and beautiful, and the town is not quite so rigid with its COVID-19 restrictions, which is a relief. Our little hotel is right across the lane from the ocean, and I wake early to the sounds of waves washing up on shore.

I walk the wooden boardwalk path south along the beach for half a mile or so, climb up a rocky hill and find a secluded bench overlooking a duck pond, of all things. I watch two egrets fishing for their breakfast, and then… three deer step out from the woods to get a drink from the pond! I never expected to see deer so near the ocean. They look right at me but don't seem to feel threatened; they just go on eating grass and drinking from the pond. It is so pleasant to just sit quietly this morning and watch them for a while.

I want to see Old Santa Rosa Chapel so we drive there, but find it closed. Soon we find ourselves wandering through the small cemetery on the property, engrossed in reading the markers—most of them from the 1800s—and wondering about the people named there, in particular the children. How did they die? And how did their parents cope?

26

Regrets

Be anxious for nothing, but in everything by prayer and supplication
with thanksgiving let your requests be made known to God. And the
peace of God, which surpasses all comprehension, will guard your
hearts and your minds in Christ Jesus.

—Philippians 4:6–7

I am the queen of second-guessing. When I have a decision to make, whatever my final choice, my inner critic tries to convince me a different decision would have been better. In the past I usually believed the critic, but I am learning that I can accept my decision and its results, and move on. Hopefully I learn from any mistakes and make better decisions going forward.

I am also very familiar with regret. I have plenty of it. I can sometimes shut it down with facts, but if that doesn't work, I'm finding that giving myself grace is the only way to move forward.

One day after we brought Joe home from the hospital for the last time, I left him sitting in his wheelchair for a few seconds while I retrieved something from the bathroom—I was horrified to find him lying motionless on the floor when I returned. He seemed unhurt, but it required two of us to get him back into his bed, as I wasn't strong enough to do that on my own.

The next time I had to step out while he was sitting in the wheelchair, I made sure he was buckled in, a blanket tucked around his lap. Once again somehow he fell out! You can't imagine my remorse and self-anger! I am still baffled as to how that happened, but I will never forget my anguish. Any confidence I had as a caregiver disintegrated with that fall, and I was heartsick over my own ineptitude.

I made a mistake leaving Joe alone in his wheelchair, twice. It was literally less than a minute each time, but it was too long. I didn't realize just how quickly he had declined that week, that he had zero upper-body strength in addition to having lost the use of his legs, and that his awareness of his surroundings was probably greatly compromised by that time.

I will never forget, but with God's help I may find the grace to forgive myself. I am realizing it is necessary to face our mistakes so they don't linger menacingly in our subconscious. To take responsibility, make it right if we can. But then we need to forgive ourselves. Emotional survival includes giving ourselves grace, and accepting that we are fallible.

One day in late 2016, Joe and I were volunteering at the local food distribution center. He stepped into the walk-in refrigerator to gather more supplies and stumbled and fell, bumping his head. He stood up, assured us his head was fine and directed our attention to the bleeding cut on his hand.

We mentioned the fall at his doctor visit later that week and they ran a scan, which showed "no apparent damage." Still, it was just a few months later that his tumor "woke up" and grew aggressively, necessitating a resection surgery in April of 2017. Did the fall cause further tumor activity? It is a haunting thought, and could crush me with guilt if I let it. I'm the one who drove him to the center and worked alongside him.

But I know Joe: If he had known he would fall and damage his brain, would he have done anything differently, such as *not* volunteered at the food center? I strongly doubt it. By then Joe was sure of his purpose: to honor God by serving people, and he was determined to serve in any way possible for as long as he could.

Since Joe died, I have had the following conversations with my inner critic:

1. *I should have more vigorously pursued clinical trials (or a different diet, or treatment at a different cancer center, etc.).*

You did the best you could with the information and opportunities you had at the time.

You did hundreds of hours of research and Jeff had major input and opinions as well; ultimately everything was Joe's decision, not yours.

Other cancers respond well to certain treatments; there is no truly effective treatment for glioblastoma—it adapts to whatever you throw at it. That's why oncologists and naturopaths alike consider it a "beast". (For those reading this who are dealing with the beast, research is ongoing. Don't lose hope!)

And this is hard to take, but: Joe was not determined to live a long life; he didn't seem to mind the prospect of dying.

2. *Wish I had provided more physical comfort. He was always chilly; we should have kept the heater turned up.*

He would have known other people in the house were uncomfortably hot and he would NOT have liked that—he would never want to be responsible for someone else's discomfort.

He didn't mind wearing his comfortable jacket or fleece vest around the house. He also ran a space heater in his bedroom, remember?

3. *I should have spent more time with him.*

Besides all the driving to and from appointments, you read to him often, played cards and chess with him, went for walks with him, and got out your guitar to jam with him many evenings, even when you didn't feel like it.

You were tired.

He liked solitude, same as you.

4. *I wish we could have remodeled the garage into a studio for him, like he wanted.*

That would have been a major expense, and you had other expenses that took priority.

His bedroom was basically a studio; he had mics and speakers and LogicPro, and everything he needed to record himself or other family members.

Eventually you most likely *would* have helped him start his own studio, either as part of the house or at another property, if he had decided that was to be his vocation. That's the kind of parents you are.

Two voices: one condemns, the other gives grace. I must continually choose which one to listen to.

27

Making Progress

Trust in the LORD with all your heart and do not lean on your own understanding. In all your ways acknowledge Him, and He will make your paths straight.

—*Proverbs 3:5–6*

Peter and Jamie took Jeff and me out for dinner tonight—restaurants are still closed for indoor dining but this one had tables set up in the parking lot and they were serving from their regular menu. We had a good time with the kids. Then Jamie went on to a rehearsal at church while Peter came over to the house—to talk to Jeff about marrying Jamie! Jeff gave his blessing. We love Peter and think he and Jamie are great together.

After several months of hot days we are finally enjoying fall weather this week: cool gray mornings and pleasant sunny afternoons. Tomorrow night we have reservations at Pizzaioli to celebrate my birthday as a family. This restaurant has a nice patio, and the weather is pleasant, so it is not a hardship that indoor dining is still off-limits in California. I haven't yet decided what to do *on* my birthday. With COVID-19 still an issue, many of my favorite businesses remain closed (movie theatres, bookstores) and we have to wear masks in stores and public buildings. Maybe I'll just hole up in my bedroom with takeout and a movie.

I practiced on Joe's drum kit again the other day and am remembering some of what he taught me. I imagine him sitting there coaching me—he was a good teacher. He explained things well and knew how to break down a concept into small doable tasks. He also seamlessly blended encouragement with challenge—he made learning fun and rewarding. I hadn't practiced in a long time, and that disappoints me. I could have been much further along if I'd kept at it. Maybe I'll start up again. I sure miss my boy...

I am still trying to write. I am working on a little book of advice as a Christmas gift for the girls. I continue to write posts for my blog at joefischermusic.com, and am finishing up a little parenting book I mostly wrote years ago but never published. I still have a short attention span and get distracted and restless easily, so my progress is quite slow. When I don't know what else to do, I make a cup of tea. The ritual provides a kind of reset, a moment to think about the task at hand and to plan what I will do next...

Finally, the large bookstore-café in our town is open for business. As I write this, I am sitting at a table there, my iced decaf mocha before me. At the table next to me are four middle-school girls, playing a game that has them screeching and laughing, even as they shush each other (loudly, as in "SSHHHHH!"). I am simultaneously annoyed and charmed. They are distracting, certainly, but they are also happy and thoroughly enjoying each other's company, and it is satisfying to witness their happiness. They may be oblivious to the noise they are making, or they may not care. Either way, today I am fine with it, and I realize what a relief it is to not be walking around in that "nerves-on-edge" haze that was my constant companion not long ago.

But the holidays are here once again, still a difficult time for me. The subtle ache returns and I have the familiar urge to retreat alone. It takes much effort to interact with people, even those I love, and I'm not sure I have the emotional energy to plan and execute fun celebrations.

Yet with Peter and the girls doing much of the work, we are planning to celebrate both Thanksgiving and Christmas at home this year. This will be our first Thanksgiving dinner at home since Joe died (we have gone out to dinner the past two years), and our first Christmas dinner at home as well. We were home for Christmas morning last year after cancelling our Laguna Beach plans at the last minute, but for dinner we were guests at Peter's mom's home. We are still marking "firsts" even three years after Joe's death.

I will try to be happy and participate in the festivities, for the sakes of my family members. I heard a speaker say recently that we each have a responsibility to be happy if it is possible, because our drab moods pull others down; if we are consistently unhappy we should seek help. Sometimes being happy is just not possible for a time, but I definitely understand his concept, as I have experienced both sides of that issue many times.

This year we pull out the Christmas decorations; I even hang the ornaments on the tree myself as everyone else has obligations elsewhere that week. On Christmas Day Peter comes over mid-morning and we all exchange gifts, then cook a festive breakfast together. We clean up, then rest for a while before an early dinner. I make a standing rib roast while the kids take care of most of the side dishes. Everything is delicious, and we have a pleasant time around the table.

Once again Jeff reads to us from the gospel of John and the book of Isaiah: "In the beginning was the Word, and the Word was with God, and the Word was God... And the Word became flesh, and dwelt among us... Surely our griefs He Himself bore, and our sorrows He carried... All of us like sheep have gone astray, each of us has turned to his own way; but the LORD has caused the iniquity of us all to fall on Him... But as many as received Him, to them He gave the right to become children of God, even to those who believe in His name."

Regardless of my emotional state, there is always reason to celebrate Christmas: we celebrate because the Almighty God has come to us and revealed Himself to us, that we might know Him and be called His friends. What an amazing, incomprehensible gift.

Bit by bit we are finding our way. God has been gracious to me, surrounding me with a loving family. They are patient and supportive while working through their own grief and healing process. I hope I am being supportive of them as well.

28

A Wedding!

For You have been my help,
and in the shadow of Your wings I sing for joy.
My soul clings to You; Your right hand upholds me. —Psalm 63:7–8

Another spring. I can go many weeks at a time now feeling almost normal, but I feel Joe's absence keenly these days... I think perhaps all the wedding planning highlights the fact that Joe isn't here to enjoy all of this. He would have been a great help—running errands and such. He probably would have written a wonderful song for the occasion. And he would have looked dapper in a suit! I'm sure he would admire Peter and they'd have great conversations. Jamie and Peter plan to dance to one of Joe's songs at their wedding—what a lovely way to honor him on their special day.

I miss Joe's voice. I really wanted to hear his voice the other day, so I scrolled as far back as I could on my phone to see if there were any voice mails from him. I couldn't find any. The list only goes back a few years and he generally didn't leave messages during his cancer journey—it took too much energy, and he couldn't always think of the words he wanted. So I don't think I have any voice messages from him.

But I do have videos! I spent a couple of hours the other day going through family videos on my laptop. I loved watching and hearing him teach Anna about changing the oil in the car, and hearing his deep laugh as he played cards with the family. He didn't love having his picture taken or having the video camera pointed at him, but he was usually a good sport, and I am thankful for that. The photos and videos are sort of a lifeline to me as I hang on to my memories of him.

And of course we have his music. He only recorded a small fraction of the songs he wrote, and each one is a treasure to me.

I finally finished my first quilt the other day, a Christmassy lap quilt. I've hung it over the small sofa in Joe's room for now. I started a quilt with a bee motif for my sister Lynn (she raises bees) and am enjoying the process more, using a pattern this time instead of making it up as I go.

Jeff and I are teaching another four-week New Members class at church. We work well together, and I am glad for the opportunity to serve with him in this capacity. Our congregation is still meeting outside for the main church service because of pandemic-related regulations. Last Sunday the "Santa Anas" (strong, hot, dry winds) joined us and blew down some of the huge tents we sat under for shade, so the staff had to quickly remove them. The sun beating down gave me a bad headache, and when I got home I took the last of Joe's pain medication. I couldn't bring myself to throw away the bottle, so I will keep it. It is a connection to him, and I have no wish to disconnect any more than I have already been forced to.

It is wedding month! I give a bridal shower for Jamie at the house; about twenty friends come and we have a great time. I have lots of help: Anna takes care of day-of setup, serving, and cleanup, and fills the role of co-hostess. Jamie's roommate Bekah and her mother Marie help with food, Jamie's other roommate Natalie and her mom Linda pick up balloon bouquets for me. I am so grateful for their help; as much as I love the idea of hospitality and enjoy having people over, I am not a natural at entertaining. I am easily drained, especially when out of my routine.

At the shower, photos of Peter and Jamie play in a loop on the TV screen, and a music playlist of Sinatra and similar classic pop songs fills the living room and back patio. Kelle, our women's ministries director, shares a short but meaningful devotional in the form of a letter to Jamie. We eat and drink, play a couple of simple games, and Jamie opens her lovely gifts.

A few nights later, Peter's family arrives from Kansas and joins us for a taco dinner on our back patio. They are fun company and graciously move the conversation forward when I, embarrassed, bring out the forgotten chips and guacamole as the meal is ending! My sister Lynn arrives from Indiana the same night; she and her son Ben will be staying with us for a few days and attending the wedding.

The day before the wedding, Peter's mother Diana and I get our nails done together. The next morning, we meet at a salon, along with Peter's sister Stephanie, to have our hair done. I am splurging and having my makeup done as well. The makeup artist finishes her work and proudly hands me a mirror. As I gaze at my reflection, I freeze in horror. I look like a clown.

I hold back tears as I thank her and pay her, say quick goodbyes to Diana and Stephanie, and hurriedly make my escape. This is not the way I want to begin my daughter's wedding day—frazzled and disappointed.

Arriving home, I duck into the bathroom before anyone can see me, dampen a washcloth, and remove about fifty percent of the eye makeup and all of the lipstick. Much better. I redo my lipstick and touch up everything else, and I finally feel presentable.

Jamie and her bridesmaids are in the next room happily helping each other get ready, and I manage a quick attitude adjustment. God has been good to us, and I am so thankful he brought Peter into our lives at just the right time. It is certainly a day for celebration, and I move into the afternoon with happy anticipation.

As we arrive at the garden wedding venue, I notice the small table at the back of the seating area which holds a framed photo of Joe with his guitar, and another one of Peter's late father. A printed sign reads, "In Loving Memory". I am touched by this gesture.

The outdoor wedding ceremony is lovely, officiated by Pastor Brian and Pastor Robbie. Jamie is a beautiful bride. The weather is perfect; the late-afternoon sun shining right into the eyes of the groomsmen, who look quite fashionable in their suits and sunglasses.

We spend the next few hours eating, dancing, and celebrating outdoors as dusk falls and twinkle lights and candles illuminate the night. Anna as maid of honor gives a wonderful toast, which elicits both laughter and tears from family and guests. Her mention of Joe is a poignant reminder of his absence, but we are all glad he is remembered on this special day.

Joe often shows up in my dreams. Sometimes he is a main character, other times his existence is merely acknowledged in my story. Recently I dreamed I was riding a bicycle along the shoulder of a freeway, headed to the hospital where Joe was being treated, but I became disoriented and had no idea which way to go. Nothing looked familiar. I also couldn't remember the name of the hospital. I stopped in a little turnout on the shoulder, and there were about eight or nine other people (mostly men from a biker gang, I think) milling around, preparing to leave. I felt a bit vulnerable and stayed near a mom-adult daughter duo, who didn't acknowledge me. Once every-one took off, I realized someone had stolen my bicycle. I was stranded... I started walking along the freeway just to head somewhere.

I don't know anything about dreams. Are they just random and mean-ingless images? I am tempted to think they tell us something of what we are feeling in real life, but if that's true, what does that dream tell me? As far as I know, I do not feel abandoned in real life; I am surrounded by sup-port. I do like the end: I didn't sit down and give up, I headed off down the road. Perhaps it's just a reminder to me: in spite of any anxieties about the unknown, just do the next thing. Yes, I think I'll go with that interpretation.

Jeff and I will be teaching the New Members class at church again for the next four weeks, then we will leave on our Retirement Road Trip! Santa Fe, Carlsbad Caverns, Fredericksburg, TX, Nashville, then Indiana to visit Lynn and Tony, Mt. Rushmore, Jackson Hole, WY... I am looking forward to the adventure.

On Saturday Peter and Jamie and Anna come over to celebrate Joe's birthday, as we do every year at the end of August, with pulled pork sliders, slaw, and peach pie (I think this is the best pie I've baked yet; crusts are difficult for me, but this one works). Afterward, the girls and I have a jam session in Joe's honor: Anna and I take turns on guitar, Jamie and I switch off on the piano, and we all sing. It has been a long while since we've sung together; we harmonize well and have a lot of fun singing everything from classic hymns and contemporary worship songs to Broadway and pop hits. Jeff and Peter are a supportive audience.

When I was fourteen, my dad bought me a used twelve-string guitar and my sister Lynn taught me a few chords. For the next sixteen years I played and sang at youth group events, retreats, weddings, and in church services.

When my mom died—I was thirty, much too young to lose a moth-er—, I suddenly found that in my grief I had no singing voice. I could not make my throat cooperate or push the notes out of my mouth. It was over a year before I could sing again.

The same happened after Joe died. I could not sing. I tried, in private, to sing worship songs but all I could manage was something resembling a cross between whispers and croaks. I found this both discouraging and intriguing. I still haven't recovered my voice completely, but when my daughters are singing, I can now happily join in. I prefer singing with them anyway; I like the harmonies.

The Caldor fire is burning (200,000 acres so far) very near our family cabin in South Lake Tahoe; we are anxiously watching the news. We have had several big fires in California this year; I wonder whether that has any bearing on why my headaches seem more frequent lately.

The cabin is a nine-hour drive from our home, so I don't get up there as often as I would like. But it has provided many happy memories for us over the years, as well as a couple of harrowing ones.

When Jamie was four years old and Joe was one, Jeff and I decided to take the kids up to join my Dad and my brother at the cabin for Thanksgiving. We had a nice visit, and Jamie loved discovering snow. On the way back down the mountain it began to snow, hard. The wind picked up, fog rolled in, and we could only see about two feet in front of us. During the hours-long descent, all four snow chains on the tires snapped off. We found ourselves slipping and sliding in a long line of cars going about two miles per hour down a winding mountain road. The few snacks I had brought for the trip were soon gone. The kids were troopers, but they were cramped in their car seats and hungry. We made it home safe after about sixteen hours of driving (stopping for the night in Bakersfield), but after that grueling and stressful experience, Jeff declared we would not be going to the cabin over Thanksgiving weekend again. I wholeheartedly agreed.

We returned, though, to the cabin many times over the following years, in various seasons. Sometimes it was all five of us, other times I drove the kids up (Jeff is more of a big hotel kind of guy than a little-cabin-in-the-woods guy). Occasionally the kids brought along friends.

The cabin is where my dad taught his grandkids to play poker, his favorite game. The river down the street is where I taught my kids to skip stones on the water. Nearby Taylor Creek is where hundreds of bright orange salmon come to spawn every October, and my nephews and niece and I have witnessed this amazing sight. We have rented bicycles and ridden along the lake and through brilliant aspen groves.

When Joe was a young teen, I decided to spend a few days at the cabin and invited Joe to come with me. Joe was always up for a road trip (or any kind of travel) so he readily accepted the invitation.

We had been on the road all day and had just passed through Placerville, heading up the mountain, when we heard a loud BANG. I frowned and glanced at Joe. "What was that?!"

He was answering, "I think a tire burst" just as we felt the flop-flop of riding on a very flat tire. I pulled over, called a tow truck, and we had the tire replaced, which set us back about two hours.

We spent the next few days at the cabin taking short hikes, skipping rocks in the river, and just enjoying the quiet of the alpine woods in summer.

Amazingly we had *another* tire blowout on the way home! We were towed to a local tire store and walked to a nearby mall for dinner before getting back on the road toward home. Not quite the relaxing road trip I had planned, but I was glad to have Joe with me on this adventure—even at age thirteen he provided a sense of security and companionship for me.

29

A Road Trip and a Wave of Grief

The LORD's lovingkindnesses indeed never cease,
for His compassions never fail.
They are new every morning; great is Your faithfulness.
"The LORD is my portion," says my soul, "therefore I have hope in Him."

—Lamentations 3:22–24

"All set? Let's roll!" Jeff and I head out on the open road to explore more of our country. We are calling it "Retirement Road Trip" but we plan to take other road trips in our retirement, so I guess we should call it Retirement Road Trip #1.

Anna has her own travel adventure this week as well. She will be flying to New York City for a work assignment. She is young and will be traveling on her own, and a part of me is concerned for her safety, but she is smart, capable, and savvy, and I assure myself it will be a great experience for her.

On the road I keep a cooler packed with healthy snacks and lunch items so we won't "break the bank" (and our belts) eating too many meals out. Thankfully Jeff does most of the driving; he likes to drive and I prefer to be the passenger, so it works out well. I'm thinking we will listen to audio books on the long drives, but we quickly fall into a routine of listening to podcasts and jazz music.

The first leg of our trip is hot, dry, and boring, with the exception of a refreshing afternoon spent visiting Jeff's brother and sister-in-law, Terry and Paula, in central Arizona. Their area is woodsy and pretty, and we enjoy our tour of their town and a delicious lunch at a local grill.

My enthusiasm for the trip is dampened somewhat by a consistent headache for the first few days—it might be the heat, the dry air, or just being out of my routine.

We arrive in Santa Fe in late afternoon, just in time to visit the De Vargas Street House before it closes. It is believed to be one of the oldest houses in America; although the original date of construction remains in question, there is some evidence of pre-Spanish colonial building methods. Across the street is San Miguel Chapel, which we also stop in to see. I love buildings with character, especially those with history, so this is a satisfying stop for me. We enjoy Santa Fe: good food, a wonderful farmer's market, and our little hotel is pleasant.

Jeff likes caves, so Carlsbad Caverns National Park is next on our list. The "bat flight" at dusk is quite a sight: thousands of bats pouring out of the cave to hunt for insects. Leaving the park after dark we notice the posted speed limit is only 30 mph, in case of sheep or mule deer crossing. We don't see any four-legged critters (or any cars)—only desert all around—so it is a quiet, if slow, drive back to the hotel in the black of the night.

The next morning we return to the National Park and take an elevator eight hundred feet down to explore the caves.

"Isn't this fascinating?" Jeff is captivated by the otherworldly underground scene. We are surrounded by weirdly-shaped columns and eerie, green pools of water. Perhaps it was a cave like this one where Bilbo from Tolkien's *The Hobbit* found his ring of power. The other visitors are respectfully quiet; only the shuffling of feet, whispers, and the occasional drip of water can be heard throughout the chambers.

"Yeah, it really is." While not the wide-open spaces and fresh air I generally prefer, I am captivated, too, for about fifteen minutes. To my eyes, one chamber looks like another. But Jeff is a detail guy and notices, well, details. His natural curiosity means he is constantly observing and absorbing information. We spend an hour and a half wandering the caves before riding the elevator back up to the café.

We are back on the road the following morning. As we approach central Texas we finally have some light rain and pretty scenery, a relief after the hot, dry nothingness of the past several hours. Our destination for the next two nights is Fredericksburg, in the hill country of Texas. The influence of the town's German settlers is apparent everywhere, from the breweries, German bakeries, and "biergartens" to the German fine dining (I relish my sausage, sauerkraut and house-made mustard). We stay in a charming rented cottage, where a delicious gourmet breakfast is delivered to our door promptly at nine each morning.

Anna texts to let us know she has arrived home from her New York City work trip. She had a great time meeting people from different ministries and using her audio engineering skills to record their interviews for radio. She also loved learning and using the subway system to get around. Strange, Anna and I have been planning a mother-daughter trip to New York for the past several years, but for various reasons still haven't pulled it off; instead, we've each had our own first-time experience of the city at separate times.

Fredericksburg is wildflower country and I would love to come back in the spring sometime to see it in bloom. We take a scenic road out to Willow and cruise the "Willow Loop" drive—this idyllic countryside with horses, cows, and goats in the grassy fields is a balm to me; the breezy sunny weather is perfect for this drive. Jeff says it is a bit too humid for him, but I love it.

The next day we walk along Main Street and enjoy browsing the shops, my favorite being a quilt shop. Such beautiful quilts lining the walls for inspiration, and so many lovely fabrics. Fredericksburg is also the home of the National Museum of the Pacific War, so we spend a sobering and educational several hours there. My back is killing me by the time we get back to the car, but it is a great day.

We drive a few hours to Waco, pulling into town just in time to stop at Magnolia Farms an hour before it closes for the day. We practically have the place to ourselves, perhaps because it is a weekday. We browse the beautiful shops and I buy a tee shirt and a chocolate chip cookie big enough to share and last us two days, and delicious. I love the drive on this day—open countryside, ranches, small towns, rolling hills…

On our way out of town the next morning we stop in at Magnolia Table for breakfast. We skip the thirty-minute wait for a table and buy our food from the takeaway counter, to eat at a table on the pretty patio. We both have avocado toast and the couple next to us gives us the rest of their lavender-lemon doughnut holes. It is a very satisfying breakfast! I top it off with a delicious lavender latte for the road.

"I'm not going to want to eat lunch out after this breakfast—do you mind if we just eat car snacks this afternoon to tide us over until dinner?" I ask Jeff. We are both cognizant of the fact that we are getting less exercise than usual while on this trip.

"Sure, that sounds like a good idea." Apples and nuts it is, once again.

The weather continues to change as we head east: from hot, dry and dusty New Mexico and west Texas to foggy and rainy Arkansas and Tennessee. Catfish and hushpuppies sustain us for our stroll down Beale Street in Memphis, blues music flowing out from the bars. The rain doesn't dampen my enthusiasm for visiting the David Arms gallery in Franklin, Tennessee. I have long admired David's work and it is a treat to spend an hour browsing in the renovated barn that serves as his gallery and well-curated shop. I could have stayed all afternoon.

The sun peeks out just as we arrive in Paducah, Kentucky; Jeff is indulging my desire to stop here so we can visit the National Quilt Museum. I have only made two quilts, but I love seeing what other quilters have accomplished. Last year my friend and expert quilter Grace Crocker and her daughter Bonnie helped me cut up some of Joe's shirts and begin making a quilt from them. I still have all the pieces but can't seem to move forward with it—probably because I don't want to mess up such an important project...

After Kentucky it is on to Indiana to see my sister and brother-in-law, Lynn and Tony. It rains the whole drive and I am so thankful Jeff is at the wheel. I am cold and tired and have a headache by the time we arrive (it may be obvious by now I am prone to headaches), and it is wonderful to step into their lovely, warm home and sit down to a bowl of homemade butternut squash soup to tide me over until dinner. And of course, it is great to see my sister! We are truly friends and wish we could spend more time together. During our visit they introduce us to Cracker Barrel restaurant. I have never been to one, so this is a fun and yummy discovery.

Jeff and I both prefer to stay off the interstates in favor of the smaller highways and byways. I enjoy the drives through Illinois, Iowa, and South Dakota. Lots of open fields (mostly dead corn stalks, but still—all that fresh air and open space!). Cool and sunny for this leg of the trip. Iowa is especially charming with its red barns and low rolling hills; we stop at a deli for a delicious home-style lunch, then browse in the attached thrift shop. Also in Iowa we stop for a walk in the town of Maquoketa and see the house where Jeff's grandma had lived.

Wyoming is hundreds of miles of nothing until we approach the aptly-named Painted Hills. The colors and the animal life (horses and antelope) captivate us for the rest of the drive. When we stop for a bowl of chili in the town of Dubois, we ask our waitress how they pronounce the name of their town—we have a feeling it's not "du-bwah"; she confirms with a smile, "It's DU-boys".

Driving along the Grand Teton National Park into Jackson, I am in awe. The cottonwoods and aspen display their gorgeous autumn colors, the towering mountains—still sporting patches of snow—are impressive. I understand why the area is such a popular (and expensive) attraction. We spend two days in Jackson Hole, walking among the Mormon Row houses and contemplating the lives of those who settled this historic community. Just outside one of the houses I snap a photo of a baby chipmunk eating his breakfast—adorable! We drive around serene Jenny Lake, and spend the day generally soaking up God's breathtaking creation. Stopping at a gourmet market on our way out of town, we stock our cooler with chicken salad, fresh fruit, seedy crackers and artisan cheese (and a chocolate bar). Who says car lunches have to be boring?

In Utah we drive through the small towns where my dad was born and spent his childhood. My dad never talked much about his early life other than to say he "grew up dirt poor". From the few photos I've seen of his family during that time, he was not exaggerating. I wish I had asked him more about those days while he was still living. He was drafted into the army before his high school graduation and served three years, mostly in Korea. He then put himself through college while raising a family as he was determined to make a better life going forward.

In Kenilworth, Utah we discover the building that housed the "company store" owned by a coal company about one hundred years ago and run for a time by my great-grandpa. It stands empty now but seems to be in the midst of a renovation as an art space and community center, according to signage on the front deck.

We then stop in Salt Lake City to see my great-grandpa's gravesite. We follow the map the receptionist at the cemetery gives us and find the spot. We discover there is no marker for him, which saddens me but does not surprise me, given the history of poverty on that side of the family. These last few stops are moving for me as I discover pieces of my family history and stand in the places where they happened. I find myself wishing Joe were with us, to experience his grandfather's life in this way. Perhaps the two of them are swapping stories in heaven now.

Once back in southern California—almost four weeks after heading out—we stop at In-N-Out for lunch before arriving home. This has become a bit of a family tradition: whenever one of the kids returns home from being out of the country or we arrive back in California after an out-of-state road trip, we feel compelled to get an In-N-Out burger. Jamie even insisted on it after we picked her up from the airport after midnight one year.

It was a great trip but I am always glad to come home after being away.

November 2021. I am restless and unhappy these past few weeks, which should no longer surprise me; we are coming up on the anniversary of Joe's death. The despondency comes upon me before I realize why. The heart knows before the head.

Someone asked the other day how I am doing. I answered, "fine...ish" and smiled. It's difficult to answer that question honestly; I assume most people don't really want to hear that I'm often on the verge of tears lately. It has been four years—shouldn't I be further along?

I find myself more easily disappointed with people, and once again I long to retreat and separate myself from everyone, for their sakes as well as mine. It takes much effort these days to be sociable, even within the four walls of my house.

But I do remain engaged, cooking dinner each night and eating at the table with Jeff, conversing with him and my other family members throughout the week. I try to just do the next right thing. And communicating with God throughout the day is imperative for me. Talking with Him is the first thing I do each morning, even before rising, and the last thing I do each night.

I also find it easier this year to set my bad mood aside when I am out and about: getting together with friends, chatting with the neighbors, or being involved at church.

And, I really am fine, most of the time. Life is good, my relationships are healthy, I am active and productive and generally content. I just have these occasional seasons of sadness and the urge to withdraw for an extended time. Surely I'm not the only one who walks around in a jumble of contrasting emotions.

I pray in this (hopefully brief) season of melancholy that I won't dishonor God in my thoughts, my speech, my actions, or my relationships. He has not forgotten me and He has a purpose for me. May I live my purpose, even if I don't know what it is.

30

Dreams about Joe . . . and Ways to Help

The LORD is good; His lovingkindness is
everlasting and His faithfulness to all generations.

—Psalm 100:5

The Caldor fire came within one mile of our family cabin in Tahoe before the firefighters (bless them) were able to direct it away from that area. My dad built that cabin when I was eleven years old. In my memory I helped build it. Most likely I pounded in a few nails while he watched and maybe spent a few minutes varnishing the deck before getting bored and wandering off to the river with my brother and our friends.

My extended family lives in several different regions of the country, and getting even some of us together for a few days is almost impossible. But we have managed to meet at the family cabin several times over the years. It is where Joe and his sisters got to know their cousins during their childhoods. The cabin is special to us; I am relieved it was spared.

For the first time ever, Jamie will not be with us on Christmas Day this year. She is married now, and we must share her with her in-laws. Although we will miss her, I am fine with the new arrangement; I am grateful she has married into a friendly and supportive family. She and Peter will be in Kansas on Christmas Day, so we celebrate our family Christmas with them the week prior.

Once we see them off, Jeff and Anna and I drive the ninety minutes south to Dana Point, where we check in to a small boutique hotel on a bluff overlooking the ocean. On Christmas Day we eat a lovely breakfast at the inn, exchange a few gifts in Anna's hotel room, then drive down to the jetty to wander the marina for a couple of hours. We have fun looking at all the boats, reading their names, and discussing what we would name a boat. It doesn't really feel like Christmas, but I have accepted that Christmas for us will never be what it once was; we are making new memories.

We dress up and enjoy a nice Christmas dinner at a nearby restaurant; there are floor-to-ceiling windows for a view of the ocean. It is gray and drizzling when we arrive, but the sunset a few minutes later is breathtaking, and of course that makes us think of Joe and how he loved a good sunset.

I have had two dreams about Joe recently. In the first, I am sitting up on a twin bed in an unfamiliar room, Joe is sitting on the next bed, and Jeff, Jamie, and Anna are standing off to the side. There are two or three technicians examining something electronic that is set into the wall—a sound system? They keep saying things like, "Wow, who fixed this? We couldn't figure out the problem. Whoever did it really knew what they were doing." It was Joe who fixed it, but he wasn't saying so (typical of him; he rarely took credit for anything), so I and the rest of the family assured them it was Joe.

The other dream is a bit vague in my memory, but the scene that remains with me is he looks to be around seven or eight years old; I find him sitting (hiding?) in a closet surrounded by stuffed animals. I have a vague fear that he may be leaving soon. I am overcome with emotion and I tell him, "I love you so much, Joe." I cannot find the words to convey the depth of what I feel for him, so those will have to do. He looks at me and says earnestly, "I love you, too, Mom." It seems imperative to him that I know. When he talks he seems much older and more confident than his age suggests. I love the dream and think about it often, because I sometimes wonder how he felt about me. For much of his life he wasn't especially demonstrative with affection. This dream is a comfort to me.

The longer we live the more likely it is we will have a friend or family member who is grieving a great loss. In our effort to comfort our grieving friend, we may flounder in trying to decide how best to express our support. We each process grief in our own way, and what blesses one person may irritate another. (Some people consider flowers a waste or a nuisance, but I love them!).

So how do you decide what to do and say? You can, of course, just ask the person what they would like, but that doesn't always work, as it puts pressure on the grieving one and it's a bit awkward for them to reply, "well, um…I like flowers…"

I think it helps to consider the person's personality, or ask someone close to them what they might want or need. And if you are a Christian, ask God for ideas. I know He enjoys helping His own.

These are a few things that blessed me in the months following Joe's passing:

Offers to do specific errands ("I'm heading to the grocery store today—can I pick up anything for you?"). I *really* didn't want to deal with the tedium of life or have to talk to strangers, so this was much appreciated.

My Adult Fellowship class hired a woman to clean my house. Twice!

A card with a personal, hand-written note—I read those over and over and they reassure me that other people miss Joe, too, or wish they'd known him, or at least are hurting for me. I have saved them all.

I loved receiving flowers and gift cards.

Hot, home-cooked meals delivered. I didn't have the energy or the motivation to plan, shop and cook. My church organized a Meal Train; my neighbors and other local friends took it upon themselves to serve us in this way, too.

Phone texts. I hate talking on the phone, but a text from a friend was often just the encouragement I needed. Texts reminded me that I was not alone, especially as time went on and the meals and cards stopped coming.

Offers to get together for coffee or lunch, but with no pressure to do so. ("When you're ready, I'm here").

My friend Jan and I went for a walk in the park; it was wonderful to be in the midst of quiet nature while we talked.

An anonymous donor set up a scholarship fund for Biola University's Music Department in honor of Joe, to help promising music students develop their talents in music (Joseph Fischer Memorial Scholarship Fund).

Our friend Jim has sent a hand-written note each year on the anniversary of Joe's death to let us know he remembers… What a thoughtful gesture.

These days—four years since he left us—it means so much to me to know people remember Joe and to hear them talk about him. I know the world keeps turning and life has moved on for everyone else, but my family and I will always have this element of sadness with us, wherever we go and whatever we do. To know Joe is not forgotten is probably the best gift of all.

31

Why?

You will make known to me the path of life;
in Your presence is fullness of joy;
in Your right hand there are pleasures forever.

—Psalm 16:11

Perhaps the most painful question I've been asked is, "Do they know what caused it?" I understand the curiosity that would prompt someone to wonder such a thing. But even if I knew what caused a fatal brain tumor to grow in Joe's head, why would I want to dredge up possible mistakes made by us, by Joe, or by doctors during his lifetime?

"To help others avoid it," one might reply. Perhaps if I had an analytical mind, and a curious personality, and if I were brave enough (and magnanimous enough), I might dive into researching the "why". But I am not that type of person. Like Joe, I take life as it comes, and keep moving forward. I dislike looking back, because once I start down that road the questions in my own mind are relentless.

Did I eat something wrong when I was pregnant with him? Did we let him play in the wrong sandbox? Did he hike in the wrong area as a teen? Did we not take seriously enough the headaches he had as a little boy when he got hungry or socially exhausted? Did he drink tainted water? If it was a genetic problem, where and in whose family line did the genes go bad? And why? I could go on and on, descending into a miry pit of whys and what ifs. But I don't. My son died of brain cancer and I can't fix it.

In a more theological vein, some people are surprised to find that I've never angrily asked, "Why, God?!" Frankly, it never occurred to me to demand a reason from God for Joe's cancer. I do not think God owes me an explanation. Since I believe in His sovereignty, I have to believe Joe's life and death serve a higher purpose than what we can comprehend. The pain I feel in missing him does not negate my confidence in God's goodness and wisdom. Some things are not for me to know, and I have a strong hunch this is one of them.

Although, I *have* wondered why He didn't *heal* Joe, when so many hundreds of us were praying for his healing. Glioblastoma is no match for an omnipotent God. Did we not pray fervently enough? Did we not have enough faith? Or, is it possible Joe so longed for heaven that God granted his desire? Again, I have no answers, and I must be content with that.

I am not suggesting that it is wrong to complain to God or to vent frustration toward Him. He "knows we are but dust"[3] and understands our limited perspective. After all, Jeremiah, David, Moses, and others from the Bible complained to or argued with God—and He showed favor to many of them and presents them to us as examples of faith. Perhaps it is simply my personality that brought me quickly to a place of acceptance. Or, perhaps I don't yet fully comprehend my own feelings. But I believe God in His grace is helping me to move forward.

I have felt the piercing pain of a sorrow deeper than any I have known before; Joe was my son, my friend, and a wonderful young man besides. I ache because he is no longer here with me. But to my knowledge I am not angry with God. I am grateful he allowed me the pleasure and the privilege of being Joe's mom for twenty-four years. And if I *were* angry about this, I would be saying to God, "Why did he get to go first?! I've been here longer!"

It is fascinating to me that "all the days ordained for me were written in Your book before one of them came to be." (Psalm 139:16 NIV). Apparently God always knew He would give Joe twenty-four years to accomplish what he was here to accomplish. And that includes the lessons being learned by those of us left behind.

After the surgeons removed a bit of his brain tissue to determine a diagnosis, Joe gave them permission to use whatever sample they had left

---

3. Psalm 103:14.

for research. Hopefully that will move things along in some small way in terms of figuring out the "why" and "how" for future generations.

I will always carry sorrow in my heart because I love Joe and miss him so much. But I do not grieve "as do the rest who have no hope." (I Thessalonians 4:13). For His own eternal reasons, which so far He has not shared with me, God moved Joe to his eternal—and infinitely better—home earlier than we would have chosen. From my point of view, there is "No Good Reason" for the cancer that took Joe's life. God continually asks that I trust Him, even when He gives no explanation.

Years ago, when Jamie was four, a longtime dream of mine came to fruition when we began homeschooling her. I loved perusing homeschool catalogs and there was one in particular that was several hundred pages long. That catalog became my favorite bedtime reading, much to Jeff's amusement. I would climb in bed with a cup of tea on my nightstand and read—not browse or skim, but read—several pages of the catalog, circling resources I wanted to try.

Two more children came along and I homeschooled for several years, loving our nature walks in the local woods, reading great books together, and generally feeling grateful for my life. However, when they were nine, six and two, I began to experience exhaustion and depression, and eventually I sensed the Lord asking me to give up homeschooling. I was devastated, and I admit I wrestled with Him for many months—hanging on to my "homeschool mom" identity for dear life— before finally giving in and saying through tears: "My children are yours, Lord. Do what you will." And I relinquished control. Or rather, the illusion of control.

We enrolled Jamie and Joe at a small local school and arranged for two-year-old Anna to play two mornings a week at my neighbor's house. The first morning I was alone in my house I sat quietly and soaked up the solitude for almost an hour before continuing with my day. I hadn't realized just how much I needed this break. I missed my children and I missed homeschooling, but I knew this time off was necessary.

I spent many months poring over the book of Psalms, which remains one of my favorite books in the Bible because it meets me right where I am. The psalms give me permission to feel what I feel, and they put words to my feelings when I have no words of my own. I read and re-read the whole book, many times praying the words I was reading:

The LORD is close to the brokenhearted and saves those who are
crushed in spirit. Psalm 34:18

The LORD is my shepherd,
I don't need anything more.

He makes me rest in green pastures;
He leads me beside quiet waters.

He restores my soul and refreshes me . . .

Even though I walk through the valley of the shadow of death,
I fear no evil, for You are with me;
Your rod and Your staff, they comfort me...

Surely goodness and mercy will follow me all the days of my life,
And I will dwell with God forever. From Psalm 23[4]

I love the LORD, because He hears my voice and my cries for help.
Because He has inclined His ear to me, therefore I will call upon Him
as long as I live.
Psalm 116:1, 2

After a year of rest and medical care for me, during which I was able to write several songs and record a lullaby album with a few musician friends, I sensed the Lord telling me I could bring the kids back home, which is what they wanted, too. Jeff, bless him, was supportive; he generally deferred to me in matters of educating the children. We finished their education from home, eventually outsourcing high school math to a teacher more adept in that subject.

I believe this was one of several experiences God has used to teach me to hold everything loosely. It will be a lifelong effort, but I am continually learning to relinquish control of anything I hold dear. Until I loosen my grip on the thing I think I must have, I will not have peace. I must trust Him with each of my children. I must trust Him with my marriage, my job situation, my finances, my health, my living situation ("Please God, move us to a beautiful piece of land with room for a cow and some goats!"), and everything else that matters. My goal is to submit to His will in all things; when He says "no" to my request, I want to trust that His plan is ultimately better

4. Personal paraphrase.

than mine, even if I can't imagine how. This is difficult, but not complicated. I simply ask myself: *Is He trustworthy or is He not?* Either He is or He isn't.

Holding everything loosely does not mean I stop caring. On the contrary, I am regularly on my knees in prayer on behalf of my loved ones and the circumstances that concern me. Rather, it means I release the illusion that I am the one in control.

These days I am aware I am moving forward. The yearning for a months-long solo retreat is rare to non-existent. In fact, when I took a solo weekend away recently, I really missed my husband and my routine, and returned home sooner than I'd planned! God continually reminds me that people and relationships are worth the investment of time and energy. My desire for solitude now is probably greater than my need for it.

I (usually) enjoy chatting with people in line at the grocery store and catching up with acquaintances at church— "small talk" is no longer excruciating; often it is even pleasant and rewarding.

After over two years of living with no pets, Jeff and I recently adopted a border collie mix from the local shelter. Ivy has lots of puppy energy and ensures I get my exercise every day. She is smart and friendly, and the kids have assured us they will take care of her when we travel.

Joe's friend Chrissy has moved out of the area but continues to remember Joe's birthday and other important dates, as well as to remind me how much she enjoys his music. She graduated from college and I am so glad to know she is moving forward, too.

Jeff is still pleasantly occupied with serving on the Elder Board at church (now as Chairman), using his gifts of communication, diplomacy, and his love and respect of the Scriptures to serve the family of God in this role.

Jamie is now working as an administrator in the church office, supporting the staff as they carry out the many ministries of our busy congregation. She loves the office culture and the people with whom she works. She and Peter join us for lunch most Sundays after church.

Anna wrapped up two years in radio production and is looking for her next adventure. She is artistic, creative, and loves (craves) the outdoors, and finding her career niche is proving to be challenging, but she is intelligent and resourceful—I am confident she will find her place.

We each continue on our journey of healing as we move forward. The four of us are blessed because we enjoy each other. Our shared grief has not torn us apart; it may in fact have drawn us closer together.

And Peter—my son-in-law—quiet, wise, steady; he entered our lives two years after Joe died, so his experience of Joe is filtered through what we share of our own. He has proved a warm and welcome addition to our family, and his knowledge of American history and politics adds a fresh perspective to our dinner-table conversations, as does his love for God's Word.

I continue to carry sorrow, but it no longer overwhelms me. Joe's death has changed me, certainly, but it does not define me. I have pleasant days and stressful days, like everyone else.

I suspect the fall and winter holiday season will always be challenging. But overall, I am at peace. I am confident that with God's help I can learn to be content in any situation. I'm not there yet, but I am moving in that direction. I do have an ironclad assurance that Jesus will walk with me through both the mountains and the valleys of life. That assurance is an amazing gift, and suffering is one of the vehicles God has used to give me that gift.

We are sometimes sad and disappointed when an elderly loved one dies. But we are not surprised. We are accustomed to a life being about eighty years long. So twenty-four years seems a very short life…

But still, it was twenty-four years. Twenty-four years to get to know Joe, to love him, to joke and sing with him, to counsel and receive counsel from him. To inspire and be inspired. To teach and be taught. I am grateful for the time we had together, and for the privilege of being his mom.

So today I am both sad and grateful. Sad that we only had twenty-four years with Joe, but grateful for those twenty-four years.

Throughout this painful journey of loss and grief, God has proved Himself attentive and merciful. Most likely there will be more difficult times to come; that is the nature of life in this fallen world. But His "countless gifts of love"[5] have buoyed me, even in my darkest hours, and I know beyond a doubt that I can trust Him with my future, so that along with Joe I can sing:

> I look forward in the darkness
> To all the uncertain days
> I can't wait—I remember You.

What caused Joe's cancer? I don't know.
Why did God allow Joe to die at the age of twenty-four? I don't know.

---

5. From the hymn *Now Thank We All Our God* (Rinckart, 1636)

All I really know is: God is sovereign, He is always good, and His ways are higher than mine.

> The LORD gave and the LORD has taken away.
> Blessed be the name of the LORD.
> Job 1:21

Acknowledgements

Thank you . . .

to the staff at Wipf and Stock for taking on an unknown author; thanks George, Matt, Joe, and EJ for your friendly patience with my questions and suggestions

to the friendly baristas at Klatch Coffee in Chino Hills, especially Ari, who always remembers my complicated order, and to Ali and Alyssa at Barnes and Noble

to Renee, Jill, Karen, Jan, and other friends who don't seem to mind hearing more stories about Joe

to the guys in Jeff's "Book Club" and their wives, who watched Joe grow up and have walked with us and prayed for us all these many years; special thanks to Jerry Hetrick for the cool teacup logo

to Buzz and Maria Dixon for years of friendship, encouragement, and support. Thank you, Maria, for your quiet presence and strength during Joe's surgeries. You made those dark and scary hours more bearable; thank you for telling me when to eat and when to rest when I was too exhausted to make simple decisions

to my lifelong friend Laurie— thank you for your love and honesty throughout my life . . . our friendship during my teen years was a highlight of that season— singing with you in the stairwells at church (reverb makes everyone sound better!); joining you on a family road trip to Canada and making your dad stop for ice cream at eight in the morning; you joining my dad, brother, and me on a backpacking trip (along with pack mules Mike and Spike); all the overnights and midnight laughter. Thank you, too, for sharing your sister Bonnie and parents Bill and Grace with me—I have always loved and felt loved by them, too.

to the faithful readers of my blog at joefischermusic.com; your Facebook comments and encouragement these past five years have spurred me on when I wondered if I had anything valuable to share. I appreciate you all so very much!

to my brother Dave for your constant support, friendship, and advice. I'm so glad to have you in my life. The words you shared at Joe's memorial service were poignant and perfect, and your love for him has always been evident. I love you.

to my sister Lynn— I have always looked up to you and have learned so much from you. You taught me I Corinthians 10:13 when I was a teenager and it is still a great reminder all these decades later! I love spending time with you and traveling with you. What a blessing to have a sister who is also a friend. I love you.

to Jamie— What a thrill it was to become a mother for the first time! You made it fun and relatively easy, even during the teen years. Your grace, patience, and sense of fun makes our lives richer and more pleasant than they would otherwise be. Thanks for reminding me of some of our Joe stories and for valuable feedback (and encouragement!) while writing this book. I love you dearly.

and to Peter, who married Jamie— You joined our family during a difficult season—we were still grieving the loss of a young man you never knew. Thank you for your kindness and wisdom... I am thankful that Jamie waited for the right man and delighted to have you as my son-in-law.

to Anna— We sometimes differ in our tastes and how we view the issues of the day, but we share a love of Jesus and His ways; your intellectual curiosity inspires me to reflect on and confirm what I believe about God and His Word. You have a way of challenging me with such grace and respect—a rare talent. Also, you're the only person I know whose cat brings her flowers. I love you to Saturn and back infinity times.

to Jeff— I was sixteen when we met! I admired and respected you then, with all your nineteen-year-old wisdom, and although we didn't date until nine years later, I think I always knew deep down it would be you, my constant friend, that I would spend my life with. We have been through so much together, and although I have found the maturing process painful at times, I know it has all been valuable and I truly can't imagine life without you. Thanks for being my protector, my provider, and my hero in so many ways, for "rescuing" me when I thought I'd lost the manuscript, and for your patient help with my website. I will always love you.

Author's Note

For several years I have maintained a blog at joefischermusic.com about my grief journey. Sometimes people ask me if I write about Joe because it is cathartic. Maybe it is, I'm not sure. I suppose I write about Joe because it keeps me connected to him.

I began writing this book so others could know Joe, so he wouldn't be forgotten, and so he might inspire us. I also felt that since grief memoirs have helped me process my own grief, perhaps this one would help the next person with theirs.

As I wrote my story, however, I began to notice God's fingerprints all over our lives, and it became apparent to me that this is really a story of God's goodness and mercy.

My faith is not the point. My feelings about God are not the point—they fluctuate: I have felt abandoned by Him; sometimes I feel ignored. Feelings lie. But the faithfulness of God is unchanging.

Mostly, I write to praise God for his love and comfort in the midst of our suffering. I have no doubt He was with us in the fire.

Isaiah 48:10

Continue following Lori's journey at loridfischer.com

Made in the USA
Las Vegas, NV
29 December 2023

83655061R00095